Teaching in the First Person

Studies in the
Postmodern Theory of Education

Joe L. Kincheloe and Shirley R. Steinberg
General Editors

Vol. 99

PETER LANG
New York • Washington, D.C./Baltimore • Boston • Bern
Frankfurt am Main • Berlin • Brussels • Vienna • Oxford

Elijah Mirochnik

Teaching in the First Person

Understanding Voice and Vocabulary in Learning Relationships

PETER LANG
New York • Washington, D.C./Baltimore • Boston • Bern
Frankfurt am Main • Berlin • Brussels • Vienna • Oxford

Library of Congress Cataloging-in-Publication Data

Mirochnik, Elijah.
Teaching in the first person: understanding voice and vocabulary
in learning relationships / Elijah Mirochnik.
p. cm. — (Counterpoints; v. 99)
Includes bibliographical references and index.
1. Teacher-student relationships—United States—Case studies. 2. Knowledge,
Theory of—Case studies. 3. Interaction analysis in education—Case studies.
I. Title. II. Series: Counterpoints (New York, N.Y.); vol. 99.
LB1033.M546 371.102'3—dc21 98-25590
ISBN 0-8204-4157-0
ISSN 1058-1634

Die Deutsche Bibliothek-CIP-Einheitsaufnahme

Mirochnik, Elijah:
Teaching in the first person: understanding voice and vocabulary
in learning relationships / Elijah Mirochnik.
–New York; Washington, D.C./Baltimore; Boston; Bern;
Frankfurt am Main; Berlin; Brussels; Vienna; Oxford: Lang.
(Counterpoints; Vol. 99)
ISBN 0-8204-4157-0

Cover photo by Elijah Mirochnik
Cover design by Nona Reuter

The paper in this book meets the guidelines for permanence and durability
of the Committee on Production Guidelines for Book Longevity
of the Council of Library Resources.

© 2000 Peter Lang Publishing, Inc., New York

Printed in the United States of America

To My Students

Acknowledgments

In the text that follows I tried using words to paint portraits of three teachers. These portraits in pedagogy resulted from many hours of individual conversation that each teacher. In deference to keeping their identities confidential, each has been given a fictional name within this text. But they were anything but fictional. Each of the teachers in this investigation was very real. Each gave me hours of hours of insight into what teaching meant to them and how they tried to reach their students. I am grateful for the unselfish commitment that each of them made to being a focal point in my investigation.

I also want to thank those who have helped me frame the numerous ideas and construct the various portraits and analyses within the text that follows. I am indebted to Mike Martin for his intelligent comments on numerous manuscript drafts of this text. Through his insightful suggestions, Mike helped me shape and reshape each chapter. He taught me that ideas were meant to be played with. I thank Elisabeth Lloyd for showing me how philosophical discourse could be an act of the heart as well as the mind. Elisabeth taught me to how to feel the power of thinking against the grain. My long overdue gratitude goes to William Bechhoefer, who was my beginning architectural design studio professor at the University of Maryland, nearly three decades ago. It was his open mind and engaging way of listening that lead me toward redefining teaching in terms of *how* one teaches, as opposed to *what* one teaches. Bill (as he is known to many) was the first to show me how teaching and learning could be one in the same.

Finally, I want to thank my colleagues/friends Gene Diaz and Joi Gresham for enthusiastically participating in the photography session that enabled me to select the picture that appears on the front cover of this book.

Contents

Chapter One

Vocabularies Collided

Multiple Voices

Vocabularies are born. They live and they die. Take for example the vocabulary used to describe the sun's motion above the horizon. From the ascent of Christianity until the seventeenth century, both astronomers and theologians found it useful to speak about the movement of the sun in terms of a "fixed earth." Their shared "fixed earth" vocabulary was based on a literal interpretation of the Holy Scriptures.[1] For astronomers the idea of a "fixed earth" began evaporating in 1632 when Galileo affirmed the Copernican doctrine, that it was the earth that moved around the sun and not the other way around. Catholic theologians perceived Galileo's new vocabulary as heresy, and they chose to continue speaking within the boundaries that the Bible prescribed. Astronomers, on the other hand, used the idea of a heliocentric solar system to transform their work in ways they would never have imagined possible before Galileo. For them, the birth of a Galilean vocabulary marked the beginning of the end of a way of speaking about astronomy. A way of speaking that had lived for nearly two millennia.

At certain moments in its life an old vocabulary will meet face to face with a new one. Within practice environments (like astronomy, theology, philosophy, architecture, education, or other domains) new ideas and new descriptions constantly arrive. A new idea will usually pose no problem for those who speak the old vocabulary because it will introduce itself through old principles, old premises, and an old acceptable way of speaking. What is not acceptable to speakers of an elder vocabulary is a new idea that introduces itself through *its own* new vocabulary. Newly arrived words, phrases, metaphors, and ideas are foreign sounding to the ears of those speaking in old ways. New ways are often ignored, and just as often ridiculed. Given a domain's established norms for speaking and taking action, vocabularies that fall outside the norm usually die quiet deaths. But once in a historic while, a new vocabulary that embodies new ideas will pack such a potent punch it will stun those who are used to speaking in the traditional tongue.

That potent punch was felt by astronomers in that historic moment when Galileo started speaking astronomy in terms of a "fixed sun" rather than a "fixed earth." It was in that moment that astronomers had to deal with the ambiguity and contradiction that went along with experiencing two simultaneous and incommensurable vocabularies: Galileo's new vocabulary and the theologian's old one. Prior to Galileo, astronomers (as well as practitioners in various other disciplines) believed that the periodic emergence of two contradictory vocabularies necessitated choosing which of the new or old lexicons was really true and which was a false translation of reality.[2] Practitioners, who were faced with crises that emerged as old and new vocabularies vied for acceptance by the community of astronomic fact finders, believed that truth existed unaffected by human vocabularies or human descriptions of any sort. They believed that Truth existed in an eternal, unchanging state, awaiting discovery. Finding Truth and mirroring Truth through unbiased description were activities that went hand-in-hand. From this it followed that to adopt a new vocabulary was to simultaneously abandon an old one that had finally been exposed as a false description of Nature. Those who discovered new facts and invented new ways of talking about the world, prior to Galileo, assumed that new vocabularies could be completely independent of old ones. Given this assumption, they argued for the wholesale acceptance of their newly discovered fact and adoption of the True lexicon they had devised for describing what they had found.

But Galileo broke from the tradition of posing the new vocabulary as being completely unrelated, and wholly independent of the old one. Instead he created a format for describing the intimate relationship between new and old vocabularies. Galileo presented the old and new astronomic vocabularies in a fictional format: a dialogue between characters advocating for and against the Copernican system. The readers of Galileo's *Dialogue Concerning the Two Chief World Systems*[3] experienced the heated debate, the provocative interplay between advocates of the new and old ways of speaking about the sun and the planets.

Readers experienced the collision between the old and new through the voices of characters who saw the world from their particular vantage points. The three characters in Galileo's *Dialogue* brought to the reader's attention the workings of cosmological systems as they had been described by Aristotle, Ptolomy, and Copernicus. In the *Dialogue*, each advocate depended on the other's ideas and propositions to fuel that person's own counter arguments. Everywhere in the *Dialogue* each character attempted to undercut the logic and coherence of his opponent's perspectives, and in doing so sought to advance his own perspectives.

Galileo's new fictional format of multiple voices in a robust debate embodied a challenge to the assumption that new and old vocabularies existed independently of one another. In the *Dialogue*, old and new vocabularies related to one another, and in many ways relied on one another, because the vocabularies were brought into existence by a trio of human spokespersons engaged in a lively interactive discourse. The new and old vocabularies were embodied by the human characters who gave voice to each of three particular perspectives. The Copernicus character in the book voiced a new "fixed sun" vocabulary, while the characters that alluded to Aristotle's and Ptolomy's positions spoke an old "fixed earth" theological vocabulary. In choosing a format that embodied the voices of real human characters who had created various descriptions of planetary cosmology, Galileo moved away from the conventional mode of relying on dispassionate, disembodied, logical descriptions that left the reader no choice but to accept the author's indisputable argument. Instead, Galileo made use of the sense of drama that emerged when real people engaged in disputes over beliefs and perspectives that each brought into a conversation where multiple views were voiced.

The very different perspectives that each character voiced in the *Dialogue* conveyed a dynamic interplay between vocabularies. I think that Galileo's multiple voices approach to introducing his new vocabulary was a useful one because it offered readers an opportunity to find for themselves a place along the continuum of positions, rather than reading the text as a successful or failed proof. I do not doubt that Galileo's intention was to convince the reader of the Copernican view of the heavens. But, I think it is important to recognize Galileo's alternative way of presenting argumentation through the persuasive and rhetorical voices of his characters, rather than presenting the reader with dispassionate, logical proof.

Galileo's way of introducing the Copernican conception of the heavens through three characters, each of whom stuck stubbornly to his respective positions even as he heard the others' well crafted arguments for the adoption of alternative positions, made it clear to the astronomers of the time that they were faced with a situation in which neither of the opposing sides could claim victory over the others. In Galileo's story of the debate between characters contending for a viable explanation of the cosmos, the conclusion was that there was no conclusion: that astronomers were faced with somehow resolving the inconclusive muddle that had been brought on because each of them was resolutely wedded to a vocabulary that was incommensurable with the rest.

Resolving Inconclusive Muddles

In *The Structure of Scientific Revolutions,* Thomas Kuhn pointed out that at times when practitioners (of various disciplines) were unresolved about how to do their work because of the simultaneous appearance of two incommensurable vocabularies (as was the case when Galileo introduced the Copernican vocabulary), a crisis ensued.[4]   The outcome of the process in which communities of practitioners have historically navigated their way through such crises toward the adoption of a new vocabulary, in Kuhn's view, was *not* based on the fact that the new vocabulary embodied a Truth greater than was embodied within the old vocabulary. Over long periods of time, Kuhn argues, a new vocabulary eventually replaced an old one within an incremental social process in which fewer and fewer speakers spoke the old vocabulary while more and more (and eventually most) spoke the new one.

Richard Rorty has also pointed out that such vocabulary crises were not resolved by choosing Truth over Falsity, or best over worst, but rather through a process in which practitioners "gradually lost the habit of using certain words and gradually acquired the habit of using others." Following Thomas Kuhn's interpretation of the seventeenth century astrological crisis between the "fixed earth" and "fixed sun" vocabularies, Rorty has written:

> As Kuhn argues in *The Copernican Revolution,* we did not decide on the basis of some telescopic observations, or on the basis of anything else, that the earth was not the center of the universe, that macroscopic behavior could be explained on the basis of microstructural motion, and that prediction and control should be the principle aim of scientific theorizing. Rather, after a hundred years of inconclusive muddle, Europeans found themselves speaking in a way which took these interlocking theses for granted.[5]

Kuhn and Rorty have pointed to some important aspects of the history of the social dynamic that occurred when old and new vocabularies collided within certain practice communities. First, there were no clear prescriptions for how practitioners should have gone about resolving their vocabulary crises. Second, a vocabulary crisis in a particular discipline was part of a larger whole composed of many disciplines and, therefore, many ideas and vocabularies whose underlying theses about the world "interlocked" with one another. The seventeenth century "fixed sun thesis" emerged at the same historic moment in astronomy as did the thesis in physics and medicine that the movement and structure of unseen elements could explain the behavior of things the eye could see. In addition to these two seventeenth century theses was the emergence of the thesis that scientists could use certain abstract mathematical systems to predict the occurrence of concrete phenomena. Even though these different theses were particular to their individual disciplines, they "interlocked" because they came at a particular historic moment when a new way of thinking, seeing, and speaking about the world had emerged for practitioners regardless of the borders that separated one discipline from the next.

The third aspect of the social dynamic of resolving the incommensurability between vocabularies that practitioners employed within their various disciplines was that "inconclusive muddles" took a long time to resolve because vocabularies changed as their speakers views of the world changed. And world views did not change overnight. A fifteenth century world where the earth was flat took a century to become a spherical world because those who talked about the earth, by force of habit, continued to speak the old "flat earth" vocabulary, and for numerous reasons resisted speaking the new one.

Rorty's suggestion that crises that emerged within various disciplines were resolved over long periods of time when practitioners became so comfortable with speaking a certain way that they started taking the theories embedded within their vocabularies "for granted" is a useful one. Rorty helps us understand that the fact that astronomers, over a long period of time, ultimately started speaking the Copernican vocabulary that Galileo created in his *Dialogue* had more to do with their process of talking themselves out of their "muddeling" by becoming used to a new way of speaking about the "muddle" than it had to do with choosing between which of two contending theories was more or less true. This is not to suggest that theory is not important in developing disciplinary practices. It is to suggest that theories within practices change as the speakers of those theories come to realize that their way of talking about what they do has, over a period of time, changed.

Theories of knowledge have historically been, and continue to be, an important aspect of defining teaching practices. While there has been a great deal of debate about the theoretical aspects of the interaction between teachers and their students (an interaction I call the learning relationship), there has been little emphasis on the possibility that practices and theories change naturally over time and that teacher practitioners who often do not speak in terms of their theories might be implicitly defining new theoretical directions that they have taken in creating their particular sets of teaching practices. In this investigation I found that all the teachers that I studied implicitly defined a theory of knowledge that drove their particular set of interactions with their students. The new (as well as the old) theoretical directions embedded within their teaching practices emerged through my analysis of their explanations of their interactions with their students.

The approach I took in my attempt to understand teachers' explanations of their interactions with their students began with observing and conversing with three architects who taught beginning architectural design studios. These teachers' recorded narrative descriptions of interactions with their students became the source for an interpretive analysis of the theories of knowledge that supported each of their sets of design studio teaching practices. The focus of my conversations with each of the three participants was purposely focused on their natural (and for the most part nontheoretical) descriptions of their experiences as teachers. I have discussed the purpose, procedures, and precedent for this type of investigation in an upcoming chapter.

What is important to understand here is that the interpretive method employed for understanding these teachers' theories was one in which the vocabularies that they chose as they described their teaching experiences were analyzed for their implicit theoretical content. In order to fully understand the interpretations of their narratives, I will describe the set of theoretical definitions about knowledge within teaching that were used to inform the interpretive analysis of the study participants' various approaches to their relationship to their students, and their ideas about the teaching practices they had developed within their roles as beginning design studio teachers.

The example of the multiple voices and contending vocabularies within Galileo's *Dialogue* was one example of how practices changed through an ongoing process in which new sets of practice vocabularies that initially conflicted with existing vocabularies were eventually adopted by members of a community of practitioners. Through analysis of the voices of the teachers in this study there emerged a diverse and conflicting set of theories that underlay their various approaches to teaching. My analyses of the theories of knowledge that underlay each of these teacher's pedagogical approaches drew upon a background of educational philosophy and design theory to interpret each teacher's voice. As the theoretical background that underlay each architect's description of teaching and learning emerged, the *metaphoric dissonance* (the conflicts, contradictions, and oppositions) between the metaphors for their respective sets of teaching practices become more and more apparent. The dissonance between the participants' teaching theories and practices was not meant to mark the starting points for an analysis that would, in the end, prove which was the best or most adequate among the three.

My approach to interpreting the metaphors of three beginning design studio teachers, like the Galilean multiple voice approach, can be thought of as an invitation to compare each teacher's voice to the other two teachers. This approach purposely explored the relationship between teachers' individual voices, the various theories that underlay each of their different metaphors, and the teaching practices these metaphors supported. My intention was to explore the vocabulary that each of them used to define themselves as a teacher. The focus of my interpretation and analysis was not on which teacher came up with the right or wrong metaphor, but rather the focus was on what role these teachers' personal metaphors might play in shaping new sets of pedagogical practices.

The descriptions of teaching and learning that will be introduced in upcoming chapters will be explored in terms of the educational theories and design theories that they embody. As dissimilar as design and educational theory may sound at first, both the education and design fields share a common ancestry. That ancestry dates back to the Greek theory of knowledge and design: a theory that supported educational, and design thinking and practice, up until Darwin's era in the mid nineteenth century.

A Vocabulary of Dualisms

Before Darwin's time, it was generally assumed that the design of the universe had been completed and that the many parts of the design had been built. It was believed that the various parts that comprised the universe (things like the stars, the planets, the earth) would remain in the permanent place that God's blueprint had specified. Those that believed in a universe that reflected the exact specifications of God's master planning spoke of knowledge as being the sum total of all the bits and pieces of His blueprint. Personal experience, in this view, had no place in the discovery of knowledge since the universe existed apart from the humans who happened to discover its various parts.

Those who spoke the vocabulary of *discovered knowledge* believed that the universe was a clockwork of interrelated parts that existed in a perpetual state of perfection. For them, gaining new knowledge was a matter of finding Truth: finding what had always been out there, in nature, waiting to be discovered. For those who spoke about "knowledge as discovered," one of the great attractions of science was that the scientific method subjected new descriptions of nature to the tests of independent and impartial criteria. Since the discovery of genuinely objective knowledge was the scientist's *raison d'être,* a method that enabled them to detach themselves from their work assured that experiments they submitted as proof of new knowledge were not tainted by their personal biases.[6] The result of detachment from one's own experience was that only genuine pieces of objective truth were ultimately admitted into an ever expanding body of knowledge.[7] By detaching from their own experience, scientists could produce descriptions of nature that were so impersonal and so unbiased that they mirrored nature point for point.[8]

It was of paramount importance that only objective descriptions of nature be allowed entry into the body of knowledge that scientists had been carefully constructing since Aristotle. For the Greeks, only objective descriptions were descriptions that mirrored the Truth as the god's saw it from their mountain top viewpoint. To have genuine knowledge, as the Greek gods did (or later when Christianity ascended, as a single God did), was to know the Truth. Knowledge of the world out there, the way the Greeks spoke about it, in other words, was equivalent to Truth. Or put another way, the Greeks made no distinction between the claim that the world existed out there and the claim that the Truth existed out there. Real knowledge equaled Truth.[9]

The Greek's vocabulary for describing truth and knowledge rendered a picture of the world of gods being separate from the world of humans. As a way of speaking about the world it supported the idea that dualisms (separations between opposite entities) were an inherent part of nature and human nature. Along with the idea that the gods resided on the mountain top separate from humanity below, the Greek vocabulary of dualisms defined mind as being separate from body. The mind-body duality that had worried Plato and Aristotle continued to worry philosophers and scientists through the ages.

In the seventeenth century, René Descartes developed a variation of the Greek vocabulary of dualisms in which he described in detail how it was possible to resolve the paradox of the "outer world of natural phenomena" that existed in total independence from the self's "inner world of experience."[10] Those who adopted the Cartesian vocabulary of separate inner and outer worlds believed that the natural world was unaffected by ideas and feelings, and was just as unaffected by language, art, or any other form of describing one's ideas and feelings. At the same time they put their faith in science, believing they could control nature by discovering all its various bits and pieces. The discovery and description of truth, fact, and knowledge was a serious undertaking that required an equally serious vocabulary.

Mind as Machine

The Cartesian's vocabulary (their way of explaining how the world worked) originated in response to deep doubts about whether or not their descriptions of external facts could ever be considered objective and unbiased. Their worry was that subjective experience could never precisely mirror the objective world and, therefore, that they could never be sure if what they thought or saw or spoke was the truth. They needed to feel assured that descriptions of what they experienced "inside" could truly represent what existed "outside." To alleviate their worries that accurate descriptions of the world might not be possible, the Cartesians devised a way of talking about the "inner" experience of the self in terms of the mind being separate from the body. They talked about the mind as if it were a machine that could be used to objectify sensory data coming in from the outside. "Mind as machine" became the dominant metaphor that guided inquiry about the relationship between human experience and the natural world.[11]

What made the "mind as machine" metaphor so attractive to its adherents was that it resolved the problems that went along with having a body. Bodies often made mistakes. The body's sensory and emotional faculties often confused what was real with what was illusion. What looked like an oasis may have actually been the hot desert sand causing the air above to shimmer in ways that seduced the eyes into seeing a mirage. Given the high stakes project of producing accurate descriptions of the world, it was obvious to Cartesians that the body could not be trusted. But, "mind as machine" was eminently trustworthy because it completely filtered the body's subjective bits of biased data through a system of objective reason and logic. For the followers of Descartes, systems of objective reason and logic included the scientific method, mathematical systems, architectural design systems of proportion and geometry, and artistic systems of forms inherent within objects.

Although the "mind as machine" metaphor was not literally the trope that followers of Descartes used to render their version of the world, it is a useful metaphor to apply retrospectively because it captures the set of fundamental ideas and theories that drove Cartesian thought and speech. A critical aspect of the "mind as machine" metaphor was that it resolved a set of doubts about what was really True versus what was error, illusion, bias, and personal opinion. The resolution to these doubts came by way of a vocabulary of dualisms. This vocabulary was built on the premise that the mind was separate from the body. The mind could, therefore, be understood as the "inner" self's dispassionate, objective, calculating mechanism for knowing what was really real in one's experience despite the body's unreliable modes of intuition, emotion, passion, compassion, and opinion.[12] Or, put metaphorically, the mind could be understood as an internal machine that could objectify every bit of subjective data that happened to enter into one's experience with the external world.

The Cartesian vocabulary and its attendant ideas that I have described dominated the fundamental rationales behind practices of all kinds from Descartes' to Darwin's era. Practitioners within fields that ran the gamut from architecture to zoology believed in two kinds of separate worlds: an inner world of the self that is separate from the outer world of nature, and the world of the mind that is separate from the world of the body. Practitioners of all kinds talked about the outer world as having an intrinsic, timeless, universal essence. They talked about human knowledge as the search for descriptions of unchanging truths that mirrored the unchanging design of the universe.

Darwin and Dewey

The type of Cartesian and Enlightenment vocabulary that supported the idea of an unchanging, predesigned universe originated within Greek philosophical vocabulary. The Greek vocabulary promoted the belief that knowledge was discovered, that knowledge equaled Truth, that Truth was universal, and that Truth mirrored the unchanging design of the universe. With his 1859 publication of *The Origin of Species*,[13] Darwin challenged the Greek vocabulary (and the later Cartesian vocabulary), in which Truth equaled knowledge, by challenging the idea that the world and its creatures could be explained by the fact that the world existed as an unchanging design. Darwin's theory of evolution was constructed, in part, on the premise that the world and its creatures were constantly changing.

Change, Darwin reported, manifested when the natural environment in which animals resided "selected for" or "selected against" some physical characteristic that enabled them to survive or caused them to perish. Following Darwin, changes to the physical makeup of an animal were the result of a process of evolution that began when a member of an animal species physically mutated in some way. The mutation itself was a random occurrence. It happened by chance. For example, one of an entire species of Pacific finches might have been born with a beak that was long and angular in comparison to the rest of its species, who might have had small, straight beaks. What Darwin explained was that if the only food source on a certain island was a hard-shelled nut that only a bird with a long, angular beak could break open, then the island environment "selected for" the survival of creatures with mutated beaks. Or put another way: the chance mutation that resulted in the birth of a finch with a beak that functioned as a nutcracker would lead to the survival of that one mutant bird (because that bird would be able to eat the food available in that particular environment). The mutant bird's cousins, who had smaller, straighter beaks might continue to survive on an island where soft fruit was easily accessed by small, straight beaks, but they would have perished if a storm blew them onto an island where they could not crack open a hard nut.

In his 1910 publication *The Influence of Darwin On Philosophy*, John Dewey detailed Darwin's important set of challenges to the old Greek vocabulary of knowledge and truth. Pointing out that Darwin's vocabulary of natural selection "cut straight under" the Greek notion of an unchanging, predesigned universe, Dewey wrote, "If all organic adaptations are due simply to constant variation and the elimination of those variations which are harmful in the struggle for existence... there is no call for prior intelligent causal force to plan and preordain them."[14] Darwin's new vocabulary rendered a picture of the world's creatures in terms of the constant physical variation that happened to single members of a species through chance mutation, and the chance that the conditions in which the creatures found themselves would select for their survival (or select against it). Dewey used Darwin's new vocabulary of "change by chance" to redescribe knowledge and truth in a way that was a radical departure form the old Greek vocabulary of an unchanging Truth and a predesigned world.

Darwin's commitment that the world was *ever* changing, in contrast to the Greek belief that the world was *never* changing, and was fixed and final, led Dewey to reject the Greek idea that knowledge existed in a timeless, perpetual state: in an antecedent state, waiting to be discovered. Instead of continuing to use the old *discovered knowledge* vocabulary, Dewey began to speak of "knowledge made in experience." Dewey humanized the idea of knowledge by speaking about it as an instrumental process of testing and experimenting in order to navigate through the problematic situations faced within everyday experience.[15] Dewey sought to replace the old vocabulary of objective knowledge (the idea that knowledge existed prior to experience) with the understanding that knowledge was the process of coming to know within personal inquiry and experience.

Inventing Knowledge

Darwin's influence on philosophy can be posed in terms of his rejection of the idea that organic forms were predesigned and eternal. The *discovered knowledge* vocabularies of various Western theoreticians that proceeded Darwin took their cues from the Greek cosmological view of a world in which an uncrossable border separated the mortal lowlands from the god's mountain top. The practice of talking about the separation of the Greek gods from humanity (and later the separation of a Christian god's heaven from a mortal person's earth) reflected a basic belief that life was experienced as a series of dualities: a series of inherent separations. As opposed to the Greek vocabulary of duality and inherent separation, Darwin's vocabulary assumed a world where the live creature was intimately related to their environing conditions. Various twentieth century philosophers who have investigated knowledge have made use of the Darwinian idea of creature-environment interaction within works in which they have invented new vocabularies for speaking about knowledge as an outcome of human experience within immediate and particular environments.[16]

Philosophers, educators, and other practitioners who eventually adopted a new vocabulary of "knowledge experienced in inquiry" at the same time abandoned the old vocabulary of "knowledge as the discovery of eternal truths."[17] Having realized that the old "eternal knowledge vocabulary" was a vestige of an old cosmology that split the world into dualities through a rhetoric that posed separations between mind and body, between inner subjectivity and external objectivity, and between god and humanity, many contemporary theorists have advocated that we drop the Greek and Cartesian idea that only an objectifying methodology could privilege us with a glimpse of reality as only the gods knew it.[18] Instead of thinking that practices necessarily needed to be based on discovering knowledge or finding truth, many recent philosophers have followed Dewey in thinking and speaking of the possibility that practitioners could make knowledge within "ventures [that] were frankly offered as imaginative, without claiming objective truth."[19]

Speakers of a *discovered knowledge* vocabulary followed Darwin in understanding that if the world does not exist as an unchanging design (as previously thought), then knowledge was *not* something that existed in a timeless state awaiting discovery. And if knowledge was not an antecedently existing something, then the knower's purpose was not to find something called Truth outside of her experience, or to produce "true descriptions of the world." Rather, the knower's purpose was to create her own set of descriptions based on her experience of her world, as seen, felt, and thought about from her particular vantage point.

The speakers of the old Greek vocabulary, in which truth and knowledge existed independently of human existence, believed in a set of interlocking theses that built upon the assumption that the world was unchanging, static, timeless, and divinely designed. In the old vocabulary, where an unchanging world equaled unchanging Truths, it was supposed that the world existed independently of human descriptions of it. Further, it was believed that "truth" and "knowledge" existed independently of human descriptions of the world. What the speakers of the new vocabulary shared with those who spoke the old one was the commitment that the world existed independently of human descriptions of it. But the essential difference between old and new ideas about truth and knowledge was the new idea that truth and knowledge were human inventions.

Speakers of the new vocabulary understood truth and knowledge to be totally dependent on human invention and description because they understood that "truth" and "knowledge," like other words, were human inventions that served human purposes. Early twentieth century educators who used the idea that knowledge was made (or invented) in human experience started to rethink the fundamental bases of teaching and learning and to reframe what it meant to be a teacher and a learner. Their various projects, in which they aimed for the development of a set of new educational metaphors and practices, were based on redefining the relationship between self and other (or put in educational terms: the learning relationship between teacher and student).[20]

The particular early twentieth century educators who adopted a "knowledge made" vocabulary developed a theoretical set of premises that were related to knowledge and experience that were very similar to the set of premises that poets of that era had adopted in their attempt to redefine the self/other relationship by redefining the use of metaphor within the process of making poetry. In the early part of the century, poets began to redefine the relationship between the poetic process of making metaphors and the experiential process of the making of an individual self (or identity). The modern poet's new set of ideas, in which vocabulary was directly related to an individual's relationships with others, was one I found useful in analyzing the vocabularies that the participating teachers in this study used to define their relationship to their students. With this in mind, the connections between early twentieth century pedagogue's and poet's respective premises for defining the relationship between knowledge-making and metaphor-making will be explored in the next chapter.

Chapter Two

Theorizing Knowledge

Speaking About Knowledge

Vocabularies that we use to talk about the relationship between teacher and student take various definitions of knowledge as their starting points. The traditional view of the relationship between teacher and student was based on a vocabulary for speaking about knowledge that took it for granted that knowledge existed out in the world before it was discovered, that knowledge was objective, and that there were ways (methodologies) for separating out genuine objective truthful knowledge from the kinds of knowledge that guide our ordinary everyday experiences. This *discovered knowledge* vocabulary originated within ancient Greek thought and discourse and continues today within many educational settings.

With the appearance of Darwin's *Origin of Species,* speakers of the old Greek vocabulary, in which knowledge was thought to be "discovered outside of experience," met face to face with speakers of a new vocabulary in which knowledge was understood to be "made in experience." For the speakers of a *discovered knowledge* vocabulary, the world had been predesigned and would remain in an eternal and unchanging state. For the speakers of the new *knowledge made* vocabulary the world was constantly changing through chance occurrence and organic adaptation.

The old Greek idea that the world was designed by a divine architect interlocked with the thesis that the world's perfect, unchanging design could be known and seen only by the gods. The "god's eyes" thesis held that only the gods had knowledge of the Truth. From this it followed that knowledge was split into higher and lower kinds. The higher "Real Knowledge" (because it could only be seen by the gods) was equivalent to Truth and was thought to be absolutely distinct from a lower human knowledge. Because knowledge in the Greek vocabulary was equated to truths that only the gods had access to, humans had to devise objective methods for sifting out subjective feeling and opinion from true fact.

The opposition to the traditional vocabulary for talking about knowledge as truth that existed in an eternally unchanging state that awaited human discovery emerged at the time that Darwin published his new explanation of the "design of the world." Instead of explaining the design of the world and its creatures as the result of the work of a divine master planner, Darwin asserted the idea that the world and its creatures evolved through a process of environmental selection and random changes within individual members of a species. Over the very long run these "chance mutations" resulted in a species' survival or extinction. The philosophers of the age, following Darwin, reexamined traditional theories of knowledge and began to assert the thesis that knowledge was not an unchanging, divinely made truth. Instead these philosophers began exploring the possibility that knowledge was humanly made within human experience.

The philosophical and scientific theses that opposed the idea of divine intervention, in turn, interlocked with the literary thesis that emerged during the same historic moment in the latter half of the nineteenth century. It was at that time that the Romantic poets abandoned the idea that the poet's role was to wait for divine intervention in the form of a heavenly muse who would inspire the poet with words of Truth from the heavens.[1] By adopting the idea that poems were personal creations that were expressive of the poet's actual everyday experience of the world (as opposed to expressions of heavenly truth) the Romantic poets abandoned the idea that their purpose was to produce "true descriptions of the world." In asserting that poem making was not about discovering truth, the Romantics set the stage for modern poets who broke from the habit of thinking that language could be used to discover what was "universal and timeless" about the human self and the world.[2]

Borders of Stone, Borders of Language

While most educators at beginning of the twentieth century were still convinced that a teacher's work was about conveying a set of universal facts and timeless masterpieces that represented "true reality," the poets of that time were redefining their work based on descriptions of personal reality. Instead of thinking that their task was to describe the world in universal terms, the Modern poets saw their work as a process of learning to describe themselves in their own terms. The Modern's interest was not in a poem that pretended to reflect "the universal conditions of human existence," but in a poem that described the particular conditions of feeling and thought within the poet's own existence. They understood that creating a self that was "not a mere imitation" of one's parents, or of one's ancestors, demanded that one learned one's own language, not a teacher's, or a god's, or anyone else's.

By the 1920s poets who created new metaphors were no longer looked upon as having discovered a universal essence. Poets, by then, realized that newly invented vocabularies were not meant to replace all previous vocabularies. New descriptions were meant for their author's personal use. Poets started equating the creation of new metaphors to the creation of the self: a self that broke from an inherited vocabulary. The fact that some poets' particular metaphors caught on while others died silent deaths did not imply that one had discovered a timeless truth while the other wallowed in poetry so personal that it was useless. Nor did it mean that one poet was an example of the paradigmatic human whose classic qualities were to be emulated while the other was an example of a slacker whose personal flaws were forever derailing the ascendancy toward perfection. It merely meant that by chance, society, for whatever reason, saw a use for the one poet's metaphor and not the other's.[3]

The Modern poet's assertion that the language that one was born into had no inherent truth imbedded in it contrasted with the set of commitments held by speakers of a traditional educational vocabulary. The traditionalists held that "learning required that the student learn the teacher's language." Robert Frost's poem "Mending Wall" is a useful entry point in understanding how knowledge was defined within the old "student learns the teacher's language" vocabulary. The poem dealt with the relationship between self and others and the relationship between knowledge and experience, two relationships that lay at the heart of educational theory and practice.

In the poem Frost and a neighbor were engaged in their yearly work of repairing the stone wall that divided their New England farms. Towards the end of the poem Frost's neighbor commented that "Good fences made good neighbors." After hearing the "good fences" aphorism, Frost wondered if he could provoke his neighbor into questioning the usefulness of the fence. He ended the poem:

> "Something there is that doesn't love a wall,
> That wants it down." I could say "Elves" to him,
> But it's not exactly, and I'd rather
> He said it for himself. I see him there
> Bringing a stone grasped firmly by the top

In each hand, like an old-stone savage armed.
He moves in darkness as it seems to me,
Not of woods only and the shade of trees.
He will not go behind his father's saying,
And likes having thought of it so well
He says again, "Good fences make good neighbors."[4]

Traditional wisdom told that "Good fences made good neighbors." A traditional educational metaphor similarly told that the wall that separated teacher's knowledge from student's knowledge was the fundamental idea that drove educational practices at all levels. What Frost showed us in his 1914 poem was that our practice of building and rebuilding *walls* reflected our willingness to habitually repeat our "father's sayings": to replicate the language, ideas, and practices that we were born into. The force of our "father's sayings" relied on us believing that the self was measured in terms of universal "goods" and "bads." In the case of the "good fences-good neighbor" metaphor, the practice of wall mending became the universal scale that Frost's neighbor measured himself against. Only if the fence was mended, only if the wall between neighbors was retained, could the neighbor feel satisfied that he had lived up to his father's metaphoric standard for goodness.

The "moves in darkness" that Frost saw in the neighbor were not to say that the neighbor had not seen "the light." The darkness was not about what the neighbor did not know, but about his practice of speaking from inside the shadow of someone else's words. A practice that kept Frost from knowing his neighbor because the neighbor had not come to know himself. Because the neighbor unquestioningly accepted the metaphors from his father's life, his voice was not his own.

All of this pointed to Frost's understanding that the border between his neighbor and he was not one made of stone but one made of language. Frost saw that mending the wall equated to mending an old vocabulary. But as opposed to his neighbor's unquestioning acceptance of the old vocabulary, Frost's inner voice spoke: "Something there is that doesn't love a wall," as he wondered if the "good fences" metaphor had outlived its usefulness. Within the poem, the relationship between neighbors that was being enacted through the preservation of old fences was Frost's metaphor for social relationships enacted through the preservation of old vocabularies. As opposed to his neighbor's traditional view that the border between one's self and others was a given (just as fences separating neighbors were a given), Frost's new metaphor posited that just as fences crumbled over time, so would the set of old standards that defined social interactions in terms of the separation between one's self and others. New sets of standards for defining social relationships would be built when the practices of "mending walls" (or metaphorically, mending old vocabularies) were replaced by new sets of practices based on newly invented vocabularies for defining relationships between people.

Redefining the Learning Relationship

Early in the century, at the same moment that Frost and other Modern poets were challenging the old metaphoric expressions for the construction of relationships between people, philosopher John Dewey was challenging the old educational vocabulary for defining the relationship between teacher and student. Dewey's importance was that by inventing an educational vocabulary in which the body was not separate from the mind *or* from the world, he opened up the possibility of practicing teaching without thinking that there was any intrinsic difference between teacher's knowledge and student's knowledge. Dewey abandoned the vocabulary of his Cartesian predecessors who thought that a borderline at the edge of the body separated the self from the world. Dewey spoke of the body-world relationship in terms of "the interaction of [the] live creature and environing conditions."[5] He understood that experience was a borderless interplay between body and world. He dropped the old Cartesian notion of an "inner self" that was separate from an "external world" when he realized that it originated within an out-dated Greek cosmology in which a bodily world of humanity was thought to exist separately from the immortal world of the gods.[6] Once the notion of two worlds, an inner and an outer world, was dropped, truth and knowledge no longer existed outside of bodily experience.

To talk, as Dewey did, about knowledge as made within experience was to understand that our collection of human faculties, physical as well as mental, commingled and coexisted as that living thing we call the body. That when it came to experiencing some thing or some person in our life, the beating of our heart and the sweating of our palms worked in continuous concert with our faculty for calculation and deduction. Dewey's new use of "mind as process" supported the creation of new educational practices where feeling, intuition, and sensation were honored for being as useful as reason, logic, and thought.

Educators who dropped the Cartesian vocabulary of speaking about the body's experience of the world in terms of timeless dualisms (like mind and body, self and other, inner and outer world) moved toward the abandonment of an old vocabulary that supported the idea of the superiority of teacher's knowledge over student's knowledge. Their commitment to the interaction between, rather than the separation of, teacher and student marked the convergence of modern educators with modern poets: by the second decade of the twentieth century both had dropped the habit of speaking from inside the shadow of a seventeenth century Cartesian language of dual worlds and universal truths. The new theory of making knowledge by making one's own descriptions of the world opened the door to the possibility of doing education without the border that separated inner from outer worlds, body from mind, or teacher from the student.

Investigating the connection between the process of making descriptions of the world and making knowledge was one of Dewey's primary interests. By asserting the primacy of the body within his theoretical investigations of knowledge Dewey came to understand that knowledge was not an immediate, ever present phenomenon. Dewey redefined knowledge as that part of our body's experience of the world that came into play when problems emerged: when the non-mental state of immediate experience was interrupted. Emphasizing that language did not enter the non-mental space of our immediate bodily experiences, Dewey wrote:

> Immediacy of existence is ineffable...it expresses the fact that of direct experience it is futile to say anything to one's self and impossible to say anything to another... Immediate things may be *pointed to* by words, but not described or defined. Description when it occurs is but a part of a circuitous method of pointing or denoting; index to a starting point and road which if taken may lead to a direct and ineffable presence.[7]

For Dewey language required immediate experience but immediate experience did not require language. Immediate states of being were languageless. He pointed out that the Greek and Cartesian paradox of a self separate from reality disappeared when it was recognized that the border was not between humans and the world but between the human states of experience in which language could, and sometimes could not, enter. The body, Dewey suggested, experienced both spaces: the languageless space of immediate experience and the languaged space of knowledge about immediate experience. Knowledge, in other words, was one's individual description of one's immediate bodily experience. Knowledge happened after the fact of immediate bodily experience of the world, and that immediate experience was not describable. Words, or images, or any other forms of description, were theorized as being the instruments that emerged after bodily immediacy. Descriptions, metaphors, and vocabularies enabled the vocabulary-maker to cope with problematic situations that required the use of words, not the search for their truth.

In continuity with Dewey's earlier work, contemporary theorist Mark Johnson has asserted that words (and other descriptive forms) do not contain meaning, or truth, or universal essences within them. Within his investigation of what he calls "the bodily basis of meaning," Johnson asserted that "words do not have meaning in themselves, they have meaning only for people who *use* them to mean something."[8] Johnson is one of a number of contemporary philosophers who have attempted the construction of new sets of vocabularies that commit to the "bodily basis" for theorizing knowledge.[9] Contemporary educators who have aligned themselves with nontraditional "bodily basis of knowledge" theories have attempted the development of a new vocabulary that redefines knowledge and concurrently redefines the relationship between teachers and students. In this chapter comparisons and contrasts between traditional and nontraditional knowledge theories will be presented and explored. Comparing and contrasting the ideas that underpin vocabularies used by traditional and nontraditional educational knowledge theorists will be useful in understanding the approach that this investigation will take (in upcoming chapters) in analyzing theory that is embedded within narrative descriptions of the learning relationship between teacher and student in the beginning design studio.

Strong Poet

Today, speakers of a new educational vocabulary who assert the body as the basis of theorizing knowledge have dropped the idea that knowledge was something that preexisted in the form of "timeless facts waiting to be discovered." The new thesis that knowledge is completely our own (that ours is no more or no less adequate than anyone else's knowledge) stands in contrast to the old thesis that since teachers know more than students everything educational pivots on students learning the teacher's language. Speakers of the "knowledge made" vocabulary do not speak about the teacher knowing more or less than the student. Rather they speak about sharing and comparing a particular student's description of one experienced reality with numerous other descriptions, including the teacher's own.

Like Darwin, who understood that there was no inherent design to the physical structure of the world, and the Modern poet who understood that the language we are born into has no inherent truth imbedded in it, educators who have adopted a "knowledge made" vocabulary understand that the teacher's knowledge is not inherently truer, or inherently better, or inherently more useful than student's knowledge. For educators who have adopted the "knowledge made" vocabulary, the relationship between teacher and student is not about the student learning to replicate the metaphors of the past *or* learning the language of the present teacher. Rather the relationship between teacher and student is based on teacher and student sharing their individual vocabularies and voices with one another. Or put another way, the teacher and student share personal ways of making those metaphors that, like the modern poet, are a way of constructing individual selves.

In defining the relationship between teacher and student, Thomas Barone uses Harold Bloom's idea that the process of constructing a individual self is analogous to the process of making poetry: of creating descriptions of one's life as a series of continuously linked stories. Defining the teaching and learning act as a process of making "strong poetry," Barone writes:

> A strong poet is someone who refuses to accept as useful descriptions of her life written by others. Instead the strong poet is a strong story-teller, continuously revising her life story in the light of her own experience and imagination. The strong poet constantly redescribes her past interactions with the world around her, constantly reinvents her *self*, so that she may act in the future with ever greater integrity and coherence. The strong poet plots her life story toward her own emergent end and purposes.[10]

Barone exemplifies an educator speaking his ideas about teaching and learning through a new vocabulary that rejects the ancient's idea that knowledge of one's self or of the world is discovered. Instead he adopts the new theory that knowledge of the world is made at the same time that one creates his self within the world. Barone's new idea is that the self is part of a process of description and redescription of one's life story. Barone's metaphoric description of teaching and learning in terms of creating poetry points to several aspects of the new definition of knowledge-making, self-making, and metaphor-making.

First, knowledge emerges within one's experience of one's own life. Second, one's idea of *self* emerges within a process of description and redescription. The *self* in this definition is not something that is an inherent essence that is found deep within. Rather the *self* is something that one makes (and remakes) as one describes himself through words if one is a poet (but also through paintings if one is an artist, or through buildings if one is an architect, or equations if one is a mathematician, or investment portfolios if one is a stock broker). Third, that the story of the *self* is not a static story, but rather the story is continuously being revised as one undergoes new sets of experiences, and in the process, understands the old set of experiences in new ways.

Emphasizing that knowledge of the world is knowledge as it is seen through one unique pair of human eyes, Barone describes the process of constructing an individual self as "the narrative that is written as a human being constructs herself through action [that] is the story of the self." Barone writes that the self

> is constructed by a conscious human organism [and is] developed and modified over the course of a lifetime, as the person interacts with the various features in her physical and (especially) social environments. Moving forward onto the environment in accordance with personal needs and desires, the actor finds that people and things within it will respond in various and complex ways. The person will construct a coherent self-identity out of these interactions by interpreting them and integrating them into a historical unity, and idea of "who-I-am-as-one-who-acts-in-relation-to-others-in-the-world." Therefore, "I" am not some sort of existential isolate who arrives at a static self identity, but rather my identity is an *achievement*, gained and modified through a process of moving upon and experiencing a world in which others are simultaneously achieving their own identities.[11]

Barone advocates that teaching and learning be understood in terms of knowing one's self in relation to others and to the world. Knowing the world and constructing the self are synchronous processes for those who have adopted the new knowledge vocabulary. Barone exemplifies the use of a new educational vocabulary that emphasizes the interaction of teacher and student in terms of the "human organism's interaction with the world." The student-teacher relationship is then understood to be a process in which both persons in interaction with one another "simultaneously achieve their own identities."

Rather than posing student-teacher interaction in quantitative terms in which the student is measured against the teacher, the new educational vocabulary poses the relationship in terms of the self that each creates in the process of engagement with the other. The new educational vocabulary is free of talk about what makes a "good" or "bad" student because the idea that knowledge of the world is made individually diffuses the need to compare student to student or student to teacher. The new comparisons are of one's past life story narrative in contrast to one's current narrative, *and* the comparison of one person's description to another person's in terms of the process by which individual narratives are constructed, not in terms of which of the differing narratives is better and which is worse.

Master Teacher

In contrast to the new teaching and learning vocabulary, the old vocabulary supports the idea that a "good student" is not one that authors a life story, but one who acquiesces to the teacher's authority. The old vocabulary is based on the idea that teacher knows best: that learning is a process of filling the student's knowledge container with the teacher's expert fluids. In his study of the beginning architecture studio, Donald Schön exemplifies the use of the old vocabulary as he defends the "master" who uses the "suspension of disbelief" trope to drive his teaching practices. Schön suggests that the beginning design student

> must temporarily abandon much that she already values. If she comes to the studio with knowledge she considers useful, she may be asked to unlearn it. If she comes with a perspective on what is valuable for design, she may be asked to put it aside... She becomes dependent on her instructors. She must look to them for help in acquiring understanding, direction and competence. As she willingly suspends disbelief, she also suspends autonomy—as though she were becoming a child again... If she is easily threatened by the temporary surrender of her sense of competence, then the risk of loss will seem to be high. If she comes with a distrust of those in authority, a readiness to see them as manipulating her, then the willing suspension of disbelief may seem difficult or even impossible.[12]

Schön's defense of the "studio master" who defines a "good student" as one who "is capable of the willing suspension of disbelief" reflects many of the fundamental ideas and supporting vocabulary that educational traditionalists use to defend the ancient's theory of knowledge, teaching, and learning. Analogous with the Greek belief in a higher and lower class of knowledge, Schön believes that the "studio master" is endowed with higher knowledge and the student with a lesser knowledge. Analogous with the Cartesian belief that since "real knowledge" exists outside of human experience, only an objective external source can legitimize what is, in fact, true; Schön thinks an objective method of detaching from subjective experience must be employed in order for the student to gain the kind of "real knowledge" that one's "master" possesses.

Schön believes that since the students' experiences are a deterrent to learning design they must follow their "master's" process of detaching themselves from their "knowledge and values" through a "willing suspension of disbelief." The teacher in Schön's vocabulary is described as having control of the student-teacher relationship by virtue of his higher "authority." The "good student" is one that trusts in the teacher's higher authority and who trusts in the method of detaching from one's own knowledge and values in order to arrive at the higher level of knowledge that the teacher has already gained.

Following the convention that learning to design equates to the student learning the teacher's language, Schön reflects the tendency that educational traditionalists have of picturing the teacher and student in a theatrical relationship where the teacher is the director and the student is a performer. In the design studio, Schön tell us, "instruction...becomes subject to the demand that it be translatable into action...of the sort the instructor has in mind."[13] As students stage what they know, their performances are reviewed based on their director's preconceived image of how a real designer acts. Students are pictured as dependent upon their teacher's external authoritative status to validate their knowledge.

Schön's importance is that he reinstated the legitimacy of subjective experience within the design process in which the design teacher and the architecture student engaged in a "reflective conversation with their work." And while this was a step in the direction of abandoning the old vocabulary that was based on an inherent separation of inner and outer worlds, Schön went only half way. While Schön legitimized the teacher's subjective form of knowing, he reinstated the hierarchical separation between the teacher's knowledge and the student's knowledge by retaining the use of a vocabulary in which teachers' knowledge (even though it was legitimately subjective) was deemed to have an intrinsic authoritative status that gave them (teachers) the license to validate or invalidate what their students had or had not learned.

The new educational vocabulary rejects the notion that knowl edge is split into a higher and a lower type. Speakers of the new vocabulary have abandoned the idea that there exists a separation between those who possess a higher, intrinsic knowledge and those who have no choice but to admit to their status in a world of lower knowledge. Schön's old educational vocabulary, in contrast, relies on the idea that the kind of knowledge the teacher possesses is distinct from the kind that students have. As a result of the separation of the teacher's higher form of knowledge from the student's lower form, the student in Schön's portrait has no choice but to admit to lower knowledge status and acquiesce to the "master's" (the teacher's) demand that students "put aside" or "unlearn" any part of their knowledge, values, or experience that the "master" deems as not useful.

In Schön's vocabulary, "real knowledge" originates on the side of the "master" (teacher), not on the side of the young, feeble apprentice. In thinking that the teacher is privy to knowledge that the student does not possess, Schön holds to the traditional position that knowledge is a search for truth. Following in the footsteps of his Greek and Cartesian ancestors, Schön thinks that if students are to discover some truth about themselves as designers they have to rely on a source outside of their own experience. For the student, the teacher (the "master" in Schön's terms) is the external source that legitimizes what counts or does not count as true knowledge.

The vocabulary that Barone and others have developed resists the tempting tradition of turning to an official external body to legitimize what counts or does not count as knowledge: what a teacher counts and does not count as an adequate student performance. Using the old vocabulary, Schön relies on an oppositional duality between student and teacher where the "understanding, direction and competence" that the student has already made for herself can't possibly measure up to the strength of her teacher's paradigmatic qualities. As opposed to educational traditionalists like Schön, speakers of the new educational vocabulary do not think the student needs to become a child again, or that she has to abandon the strong poetry (her own description of her individual identity and set of experiences) that she brings to the studio learning relationship.

Intersecting Vocabularies

The fundamental difference between Barone's descriptions of the student-teacher relationship and Schön's description of that same relationship is the difference between the commitment that "knowledge is made in one's experience" and the idea that "knowledge is found outside of one's experience." Barone understands the student's purpose to be the making of her own knowledge as she creates her own set of descriptions based on her unique set of experiences. Schön assumes that since the "master's" knowledge and experiences are more adequate than the students, the students' descriptions (what they say, or do, or draw, or write) are legitimate only when and if their teacher, who has the special authority to do so, validates them. As opposed to Schön's educational traditionalism, Barone is not interested in whose knowledge is more or less adequate, or in what way of passing judgment is the right way of determining who is "a good student" or who is "less than a good student."

Thomas Barone is one of a growing number of speakers of the new educational vocabulary who have abandoned the idea that any one person possesses the paradigmatic qualities that make that person the *true authority*, one whom others will want to choose as their "master." Instead of talking about the interaction between student and teacher in terms of the student's lesser qualifications in comparison to the teacher's authority, Barone talks about both teacher and student engaging in a process where they individually author their own life-story and their own identity (or self).

Following the new theory of teaching and learning, the teacher doesn't think that the students need to suspend their disbelief in what the teacher says or does. Moments when the student disbelieves what the teacher puts forth are moments that indicate that the student is actively engaged in resisting and breaking down the metaphors in the teacher's vocabulary. The students' process of resisting the teacher's vocabulary is a process through which the students break down the teacher's metaphors on their way to constructing their own new set of metaphors that are, at the same time, the new description of their self.

Following Barone's new "strong poetry" metaphor for defining knowledge in educational contexts, the speakers of the new vocabulary understand that the teacher's ways of describing her world come from her particular vantage point and are not equivalent to Truth. The process of student-teacher engagement is a process in which both teacher and student listen for contrasting views, for contradictory interpretations, for unresolved feelings, and for misunderstandings.[14] The new educational thesis of "listening for the conflicts that emerge as different voices intersect" emphasizes the uses that can be made whenever there is a resistance between the student's and teacher's language. Resistance to the other's voice and vocabulary is viewed as a vehicle that can potentially move the teacher and student's mutual conversation forward.

I recently came across a monograph produced by Carol Gilligan, Lyn Mikel Brown, and Annie G. Rogers. Gilligan and her collaborators have produced groundbreaking studies of women struggling to retain their individual "voice" in educational settings. In this particular monograph they imaginatively critique the emphasis on objectification that supports practices where visual imagery is significant. They write

> visual images encourage atemporality, objectification, and a split between subject and object, body and mind. Metaphors of voice and hearing, in contrast, do not carry the same implications of separation and control, but instead draw attention to human connection—to the relationship between speaker and listener, to the possibility of different languages, and thus to the potential for misunderstanding and mistranslation as well as the ability of people to see and speak about themselves and the world in more than one way.[15]

Gilligan, Brown, and Rogers remind us that because visual objects and images (buildings, paintings, books, etc.) exist outside of our bodies we tend to think of them as separate, rather than as connected to us. Their assertion that such thinking is driven by a vocabulary of dualisms is meant to challenge traditional teaching practices in places where visual communication is emphasized (places like the university architecture studio). Their metaphors of "voice" and "human connection" assert that knowledge is made within bodily experience. Their "bodily metaphors of voice and hearing" advocate that teachers move out of the shadow of the traditional educational language in which control equates to separation. Gilligan believes that by abandoning the thought of a self as separate from the world, we can practice controlling the relationship with our students through our connections with them rather than our separation from them.

Gilligan wants to shift the conversation about the nature of knowledge (in a place like the architectural design studio where most of the teacher-student interaction is based on the making of objects that represent buildings) away from the traditional vocabulary of dualisms and toward "bodily metaphors of voice." Richard Coyne and Adrian Snodgrass are architectural educators who also support the shift from the old objective knowledge vocabulary to a new vocabulary in which, as they themselves write, "knowledge about the world is self knowledge."[16] Within their studies of architecture studio processes, Coyne and Snodgrass call for redescribing the act of teaching and learning design in terms of a "critical vocabulary" where the emphasis is on the "dialogue" that emerges as student and teacher interact with one another. They frame the teacher-student learning interaction in the design studio in terms of the teacher's interest in

> developing design ideas in the context of design dialogue; simulating the experience of various kinds of design dialogue at the drawing board; and being actively involved in the development of the design ideas of others. The skills that this may include: skills in dialogue as both designer and adviser; skills in responding to design dialogue with appropriate design actions; and developing a critical vocabulary for discussing problems and ways of designing.[17]

Like Gilligan and her colleagues, Coyne and Snodgrass are aware that made objects like building designs are often perceived as detached from their makers and, therefore, perceived as object-ifications of the subjective process through which the objects emerged. They abandon the idea that building designs are "precious objects of self expression that always need to be defended."[18] Designs are not precious, or perfect. They do not have anything deep within them that is a hidden truth, or a Platonic essence. The designed object is an expression of the maker's self, and it does not need to be defended or approved by an external authority. Rather, the designed object, for Coyne and Snodgrass, marks the starting point in a dialogue. It is the dialogue, rather than the object itself, that is recognized as the critical aspect of the teacher-student relationship. And so the dialogue for discussing the process of designing, rather than whether or not the design is "good" or "bad," becomes the basis that drives the process of learning about one's "self" and the "other."

Speaking through a vocabulary in which knowledge is made within the knower's particular and unique experience, Coyne and Snodgrass's description of the design teaching and learning process stands in contrast to the Schön portrait of the same process that I presented earlier. Their two contrasting versions point to the inter-section in which speakers of a new educational vocabulary and speakers of the traditional educational vocabulary often meet to explore the direction of educational practice. The difference between the Schön method of "suspension of the student's disbelief" as compared to Coyne and Snodgrass's "development of a critical vocabulary" is the difference between the idea that teachers' knowledge empowers them to control their students because they are at a level separate from the student *and* the idea that both teacher and student make their own knowledge (and invent their own ways of describing what knowledge they have made) within a dialogue controlled through equivalency, rather than through differences in power and authority.

The contrast between Schön's master teacher and the dialoging teacher, that Coyne and Snodgrass portray, illustrates at least two possible vocabularies that teachers can choose to define the basis of their relationship to their students. The contrast of vocabularies also points to the contrast between Schön's acquiescent, childlike student, and Coyne and Snodgrass's student as a dialogue partner. In this study I will introduce you to each of three design studio teachers with the intention of portraying the voice and vocabulary that each conveys through conversations about themselves and their students. I have pointed here to the multiple ways of talking about knowledge that are currently being used within conversations whose participants are interested in defining how design should be taught. In the next chapter I will introduce you to the methodology I used to explore how three architects whom I observed and spoke with defined themselves as teachers: how they understood their individual voice and which theoretical bases supported their vocabulary for describing themselves and their students.

Chapter Three

Metaphor and Methodology

Metaphoric Impermanence

In an address entitled "Education By Poetry," which he delivered at Amherst College in the early 1930s, Robert Frost asserted to his audience that understanding the "beauty" of metaphor was a matter of understanding that "All metaphor breaks down somewhere."[1] If we recall that poets before Frost's modern era believed that the metaphor never broke down anywhere (that the metaphor was timeless and permanent), Frost's asserting the metaphor's *impermanence* can be a way of understanding the set of traditional premises about language and knowledge that he and other modern poets had abandoned by the onset of the twentieth century. Frost's poet predecessors believed that a good metaphor was one that could never break down. Premodern poets believed that the work of making poetry was about authoring poems that contained truths so timeless that their metaphors were exempt from breakdown: that the ideas, and insights, and moral messages contained within their metaphors were eternal. The premodern poets' talents were measured in terms of whether or not their words, phrases, and metaphors (and all other linguistic aspects within their poems) contained universal truths within them. Frost's poet ancestors believed that words containing timeless essences and universal truths could be transported from the heavens above into the minds of the great poets, whose job it was to put those words to paper. Metaphors penned by great poets were metaphors that would last forever.

The idea that universal and unchanging truth and knowledge could be discovered, a popular notion within premodern cultures ever since the Greeks, made it easy for the premodern poet to think that words could contain Truth, or that words configured in certain ways could be considered to be metaphors that would last forever. As opposed to the notion that truth and knowledge were discovered, the modern poet started thinking that truth and knowledge were made *rather than* found. Having abandoned the idea that the measure of real knowledge was its *universality,* modern poets started thinking of knowledge in terms of its *particularity;* in terms of knowledge as something made within a poet's particular set of experiences.

Truth and knowledge were no longer universals that existed outside of the poet's experience. Rather they emerged entirely within the poet's own set of experiences as a description maker, as an inventor of metaphors that were artifacts of things known, and truths understood within the poet's own experience. The modern poets understood that truth was an aspect of the human activity of making descriptions. They understood that "truth" and "knowledge" were human concepts. And as human concepts they originated, just as all human concepts originated, within human thought and speech. "Truth" was made as human speakers spoke sentences in which they used the word "truth" to describe what they had come to believe was true within their experiences. "Knowledge" was made as human authors produced manuscripts in which they used the word "knowledge" within sentences that helped explain the things of life that they had come to know.

Twentieth century poets no longer pretended that their metaphors commanded the strength of "eternal Truth" itself. The strength of the metaphor was not in its truth-reflecting capacity, but in its capacity as a medium for redescribing the past: for putting new spins on old ways of thinking and speaking. They realized that metaphors, and the truths that they signified, were markers of the particular set of ideas that happen to be floating around within culture during any given historic moment. Because metaphors and the truths they signified were bound within their historical contexts, they changed as the times changed. Understanding this, the modern poets realized that just as they were born into a set of conventions, into a set of old metaphors authored by the dead poets of the past, that their own fresh ideas and vibrant metaphors would someday seem passé to a new generation. At the same time they realized that because the old metaphors they had been born into were not the "timeless Truths" that poets of the past assumed they were, there was an opportunity to manipulate the old metaphors and to shape them toward their own ends.

The process of redescribing the past was at the same time a process in which poets could describe who they were at present. Through the process of redescribing the set of metaphors that they were born into, poets could come to make a vocabulary for themselves that was not an imitation of their predecessors' metaphors. By rethinking metaphor making in terms of its capacity for enabling them to redescribe the past as they invented metaphors descriptive of the self that they were becoming at present, Frost and other modern poets began to redefine the poet *and* his work. The modern poet was redefined as a word manipulator, a vocabulary inventor, who attempted to know who he was by creating a set of metaphors that, rather than being imitations of past poets' metaphors, were uniquely his own.

The modern poet had come to understand that his work as a metaphor maker was based on his individually defined set of standards and purposes. But once an individual poet had penned and published, or merely spoken his poem, his purely private metaphors entered into a public market where they would be used as their users saw fit. An individual poet's metaphors were always susceptible to breaking down because there were always other poets who would take exception to them: other poets who would question their usefulness, their relevance, or of their being merely imitations of past poets' metaphors rather than being reflective of their author's individuality. Other poets who would handle them, manipulate them, and interpret their meaning in their own way. And through such wear and tear, any new metaphor would eventually wear thin, or over time, take on an appearance that would be unrecognizable compared to its former self.

Inevitable breakdown, as Frost and other modern poets recognized, was part of an unavoidable cycle in which new sets of metaphors would eventually replace the old. As modern poets realized that there was no such thing as a metaphor, or a vocabulary that would last forever, they abandoned the idea that language contained "timeless Truth." Having abandoned the idea that a human vocabulary was more or less adequate depending on how closely it came to matching, word for word, "the timeless vocabulary of Truth that existed out there", they dropped the idea that any particular vocabulary was the best of them all; they dropped the idea that there could be a single vocabulary that all the others had to measure up to. By the 1930s, when Frost gave his Amherst address, poets had come to recognize the impermanence of metaphor. Their new interest in creating metaphors that were uniquely personal to their individual sets of experiences had eclipsed the idea that a metaphor could be generalizable, or universal, or that among the many contenders, some one poet's metaphor reflected his discovery of "eternal Truth."

Mobile Assemblage of Portraits

Qualitative researchers who have produced works in which they have attempted to render portraits of the unique and particular day-to-day lives of teachers and students can be compared to modern poets in that both poet and researcher abandoned the need to discover universal, generalizable truths. Qualitative studies, rather than influencing the reader by presenting conclusions that held true for all cases, derived their impact through the presentation of single cases or constellations of single cases. The impact on the reader came when the reader saw or understood the character (or characters) portrayed in the study in a new way; in a way that pointed to aspects of that character (or those characters) that were previously unseen or misunderstood. The impact of qualitative investigations, as Elliot Eisner has pointed out,

> is determined by the extent to which it informs. There is no test for statistical significance, no measure of construct validity... What one seeks is illumination and penetration. The proof of the pudding is the way in which it shapes our conception of the world or some aspect of it.[2]

The qualitative researcher's alliance with the modern poet can also be understood in terms of the commitment that both had to the premise that the work of description making was not about the discovery of a single best vocabulary, but rather about comparing various vocabularies and various conceptions of the world. That commitment to "descriptive portrayals of multiple views and voices" underlies the approach to understanding the teaching practices that three qualitative researchers used within their early 1980s study of high school teaching practices. Each researcher individually observed and analyzed one of three high schools that were located in contrasting geographic, social, and economic contexts.

Sara Lawrence-Lightfoot, Robert Coles, and Philip Jackson each produced essays in which they described their observations of teachers and students within contexts that included an inner-city public high school in Atlanta, a suburban high school near Chicago, and an elite New England boarding school.[3] The organizers of the study, and the three researchers I just mentioned, understood that their comparative viewpoints would become the source of a better understanding of the effectiveness of teaching within these schools. Their different views and reporting styles were not thought to be more or less adequate than one another, but rather their different perspectives *and* different vocabularies for reporting what they had observed were understood to be the source through which the reader could critically compare one researcher's viewpoint to the others, *and* the constellation of researchers' viewpoints to their own.

The poet's recognition that metaphor making was a process that could lead to redescriptions of past ways of thinking can further be understood as being aligned with the qualitative researcher's interest in redefining the standards by which teaching was practiced during the time in which the research was undertaken. Several qualitative studies come to mind in this regard. In the late 1960s in *Death At An Early Age,* Jonathan Kozol challenged the conventional perception that the civil rights legislation of the 1960s had resulted in classroom equity through his provocative portrait of teaching practices within an inner city Boston school, which pointed to the institutionalization of racism and inequality.[4] In *White Teacher,* first published in 1979, Vivian Gussin Paley marked the possibility that racial difference in the classroom was an opportunity for white teachers to critically examine and eventually grow out of their stereotypic prejudices.[5] In *Run School Run,* Roland Barth's educational vision of honoring diversity, exploring new evaluation methods, and democratizing the relationship between teachers and principals was a stark contrast to 1980s neo-conservative demands that schools return to curricular standardization, classroom discipline, and authoritarian administration.[6]

These studies were posed as qualitative investigations. They did not follow the traditional research mode in which statistical evidence was gathered and analyzed toward the validation or invalidation of a stated hypothesis.[7] These studies followed the characteristics of describing a situation that the qualitative researcher shared with the modern poet: a portrayal of the particular aspects of a situation; a comfort with the author herself, or himself, using the first person "I" to report on what had been observed; an interest in rethinking the premises that past authors used to guide their work; and an understanding that the historical context within which the author operated was a shifting context and, therefore, conclusions were, at best, temporary.

In following Frost's understanding of the impermanence of metaphor, within my analyses of metaphors for teacher-student interactions I intentionally resisted searching for conclusions. Rather than searching for conclusions, I looked for a way to conceptualize my analytic process. In analyzing each teacher's narrative description of work done with students, I found that each of their individual approaches was in certain instances aligned with the other teachers that I studied, and at the same time each of their approaches was a counterpoint in comparison to the others.

As I began seeing the three teachers' narratives as part of one analytic process, I began envisioning their theoretical points and counterpoints hanging together in much the same way as the abstract metal shapes hang together in an Alexander Calder mobile sculpture. Each teacher's narrative in my analytical approach became one hanging element in a mobile composed of three such elements. Each of the narratives embodied a theoretical stance that was a counterbalance to one or both of the theories implied within the other two teachers' narratives. This "mobile sculpture" vision of the whole was useful in that it enabled me to recognize that although the weight that each of their theories carried was separate from the others, seen together they were part of a larger whole of weights and counterweights, points and counterpoints, positions and oppositions. As a way of moving my investigation forward, I conceptualized my analytical process as a process of creating a "mobile assemblage of qualitative portraits" that in the end would be hung for public viewing and open to its audiences' multiple interpretations.

My analyses in the form of a mobile assemblage of qualitative portraits were purposely inconclusive, and intentionally debatable. That is, my analyses of narrative descriptions of each teacher's respective set of educational practices were not intended to follow in the traditional hypothesis testing mode that would, in the end, lead to a conclusion that pointed to the hypothesis being correct or incorrect. Rather it was intended as a catalyst that might ignite the beginnings of future conversations among educators who understood that because the vocabularies that drove educational practices were *impermanent*, there was an inevitable need to continually invent, and test out, new sets of educational vocabularies, some of which might eventually replace the old crop.

Manny Bradley, Joe Constantino, and Gina Vismara were the three teachers whose educational voices, vocabularies, and metaphors comprised the "mobile assemblage of qualitative portraits" within this study. Their respective narrations about their interactions with students were the basis of my analysis of the theoretical framework that guided each of their approaches to teaching. Manny, Joe, and Gina were employed by the University of California as part time adjunct professors. Their positions as part-time, rather than as full-time, university professors pointed to their shared interest in leading a life in which they could split their time between their commitment to practice in the world of architecture and their commitment to teaching in the world of the university undergraduate architecture studio. All three teachers had an interest in balancing their roles as architectural practitioners with their roles as teachers. Because each of them had a foot in both the world of practice and the world of education, each of them was able to move freely between those parts of the conversation that focused on the use they made of their "expert" language of practice and those parts of the conversation that focused on their students' use of "ordinary" spoken language. All three teachers expressed an interest in engaging in the type of conversation that would serve as a vehicle for their own personal reflection on their teaching. In each of their cases, they took their roles as teachers seriously and viewed the process of "being studied" as beneficial in that it would help them better understand both themselves and their students.

Observation and Conversation

In the two chapters that preceded this one I presented several overviews: an overview of how theories of knowledge have historically coincided with paradigmatic shifts within science, poetry, and education; an overview of the emergence of traditional and nontraditional conceptions of knowledge within Western discourse; and a overview of current applications of traditional and nontraditional knowledge theory within teaching practices. In the four chapters that follow this one I attempt to describe the theories of knowledge embedded within each of three teachers' descriptions of their respective sets of beginning design studio teaching practices. In the first part of this chapter I explored how the literary concept of metaphoric impermanence related to qualitative research. I now want to discuss the approach I employed within my interpretive analysis of the theoretical origins of the metaphors that the three teachers I observed and spoke with used within their narrated reflections on their respective sets of design studio teaching practices.

Discussions about what knowledge is, and what it has to do with teaching and learning, have played central roles within the historical development of educational practices.[8] The relationship *between* definitions of knowledge *and* the development of design studio teaching approaches had been explored within various investigations of educational theory and practice within design studio settings.[9] But the relatedness between knowledge theories and teaching practices had not been fully explored from the perspective of architectural educators' personal descriptions because most previous studies relied on traditional methods of reporting findings from detached third person viewpoints.   One of my aims in undertaking this study was to add teachers' voices to discussions about studio education by bringing forth the vocabularies that teachers used in describing design studio experiences: to portray teachers' experiences as told through their first person voices.

My approach was to observe three beginning design studio teachers and then to record conversations in which I asked them to reflect on their interactions with students.   I did not narrow my conversations with the study participants to the topic of "theories of knowledge related to their teaching practices."   In fact, in conducting recorded conversations with each of them, I *intentionally* excluded questions about their "theories of knowledge" or their "philosophies of education" because I wanted them to bring to our conversations their own sets of issues and interests as they reflected back on those episodes that I observed.

It may seem problematic that I intentionally did not ask the teachers that I conversed with to theorize and philosophize about knowledge, since one of the primary questions that drove my investigation was "By what theories of knowledge do studio teachers teach their students to design?"   But the intentional exclusion of discussion about the role that knowledge theory played within the study participants' sets of teaching practices was not problematic because as each of them spoke with me they invented metaphors that when analyzed for their theoretical content, pointed toward the various definitions of knowledge that guided their three approaches to teaching.   By keeping the conversations pointed away from theoretical discourse and instead focused on the three teachers' teaching experiences, their natural storytelling capacities came into play, and as a result they created what Clifford Geertz has called "thick description":   detailed personal descriptions of their studio interactions with their students.[10] Following the premise that educational theory emerges from within educational practice, the starting points of my analyses of theoretical content within the three sets of teaching practices that I investigated, were the participating teachers' own descriptions of their personal sets of pedagogies.[11]

The observations that I conducted of these teachers' interactions with their design students, and the follow-up conversations in which they reflected back on teaching episodes with their students, provided me with the set of narratives that I analyzed in terms of the theories of knowledge that their descriptions implied.   My series of observations of the teachers within their regular design studio teaching roles, and my series of follow-up conversations with them, was based on my interest in documenting both their interactions with students and the metaphors of teaching that they invented as they reflected back on these interactions. The notes I took as I observed each teacher's interactions with the students, I brought into our conversations as starting points in which the teacher might, for example, talk about a particular student's learning capacity, a student's learning style, the mode of intelligence that students used in investigating design issues, the problems that students were having with learning "the language of architectural form making," or students' inhibitions about their cultural backgrounds. These teachers' various reflections on their students as learners became one of the sources of understanding what theory of knowledge underlay each of their respective sets of pedagogical strategies.

My procedure for gaining access to each particular teacher's studio began with contacting them via telephone and explaining my interest in having them participate in a study that would add to research on teaching theory and practice. Within those conversations we agreed on a time and place to initially meet so that I could personally convey the nature of the study. At our initial meeting I described my interests: observing them within their teaching roles and recording a series of conversations in which they reflected on their studio experiences. I told them I would answer any questions about the study, or their role, or their students' roles, within it. I also described my set of observations and recorded conversation procedures.

It was at the preliminary meeting that I described my interest in observing them for approximately thirty hours, which translated into fifteen observations that were about two hours in length. I described my observation role within their regular design studio hours as that of a "silent observer": a notetaker who would "shadow them" and not participate in the teaching/learning process that I was observing. I clarified that my notetaking would amount to handwritten notes on a legal pad: that I would not use any electronic recording devices in the design studio observation phase of the investigation. This was in the interest of my presence in their design studio as being as unobtrusive as possible. Of course, I would be noticed by students and by the participating teacher, but I believed that taking handwritten notes would lessen the influence on their behaviors, as compared to the option of using a tape or video recorder to document their teacher-student interactions. After regular studio hours, when I was no longer observing teacher-student interaction, I had several conversations with students about their processes of learning to design. Within these conversations students often ex-pressed their views about their teacher's approach to teaching.

Although most of the notes I took were of verbal interactions between teacher and student, I also attempted to document the ambiance of the architecture studio and the culture of the architecture school itself. These notes referred to the physical make-up of the architecture studios or the set of student behaviors that I found to be common to the culture of the architecture schools (huge coffee intake, or "pulling all nighters," for example). Some of my notes were of the details that related to the particularity of the University of California at Berkeley, where I conducted my investigation. The students' preference for the local Cafe Strada coffee shop, or the legendary view from the ninth floor balcony, are examples of particularly local details at the UC Berkeley Department of Architecture. Details about life within the architectural education culture were intended to be used within the study to convey a sense of the place that the three participating teachers inhabited.

Theoretical Place

My analyses of the three studio teachers' narrative reflections on their interactions with students were intended to convey a sense of the theoretical place that each of them inhabited. My way of conveying the sense of each teacher's theoretical place was based on listening for the various metaphors they used as they described their relationship to their students. These metaphors became my starting points for analyzing what types of theories of knowledge underlay each of their respective sets of teaching strategies.

The transcriptions of their narrations about their studio interactions with students became my document source of analyzing the types of theories of knowledge implicated within their narratives. My procedure for conducting the series of conversations I had with each teacher (during three separate academic sessions, over an eighteen month period) precedes my discussion of my interpretive analysis procedure. Each teacher agreed to participate in three, sixty-to-ninety-minute long conversations during the academic session in which I observed. In two cases the sessions were seven week long summer sessions, and in one case the session was a sixteen-week fall session. The conversations were conducted in places that the participants suggested. My interest in their suggesting the conversation location was to have them feel as comfortable as possible: to meet in places where they felt that our conversations could be more of an interchange of ideas and concerns and less an "interview" session in which I did all the questioning and they did all the answering. I met with one participant in his architecture practice office, another at a local cafe, and the third in a small meeting room where we recorded our conversations over lunch.

My overall aim in having a series of three conversations (with each teacher) spread out over the course of one academic session was to use each conversation as the basis for informing my subsequent observation of each of them in teaching interactions with their students. For example, during my first conversation with Manny (one of the teachers I observed and spoke with), he described one of his students as having made "an interesting reversal" from a "counter productive" mode of reacting spontaneously to criticism *to* using a more productive reflective "thinking" mode. Keeping in mind Manny's emphasis on reflective reasoning (as compared to emotional reacting) my observations during the interim period, between our first and second conversations, were partly focused on how Manny related to students who had not made the "reversal" from reacting to reflecting, compared to students who were reflective to begin with, or had made the "reversal." The notes I took on my observations during the interim period became the source for engaging Manny in a second conversation, which led to my understanding more about his interest in the "reactive versus reflective" modes of his students.

The example above illustrates my iterative approach to conducting the series of conversations held with each teacher. This approach can be defined as a process in which the issues and interests that emerged in the first conversation, or if you will, the first iteration, were used to inform the observations between iterations. My approach going into the first conversation was to ask the teachers about particular episodes with their students that I had observed, and to listen for their particular emphases, their particular angles, their particular vocabularies for describing engagements with their students. Within our conversations I listened for moments in which I was being told about something "interesting" that a student had done, or when one student was being compared to another, or when certain students were being described as "problematic," or when students were being remembered for the surprising "leaps" they had made, or for their "incredible abilities." I took these moments in our conversations as possible signals of the emergence of an underlying metaphor that the teacher I was in conversation with was using to describe the basis of the relationship to his or her students.

The first conversation was a sketchy iteration in the sense that it did not direct me toward understanding more about the teacher's specific metaphors for his or her overall approach because I was still in the process of listening for those moments in the conversation that signaled further inquiry. Within the second iteration, I was able to engage them in more conversation about those particular teaching interactions that I had observed (in the interim between conversations) that I felt related to their emerging metaphorical description of their teaching. My lines of inquiry by the second iteration were, if you will, less sketchy, stricter, and more solid. And by the third iteration, again, after I had used fifteen interim hours of observation time to look and listen for the manifestations of recurring metaphors that I had heard within our conversations, my lines of inquiry became more solid. In each case, with each teacher, what started as a sketchy first iteration, ended up as a well delineated iteration by the third conversation.

For example, Manny, who early on described his interest in a "reflective versus reactive" students, in our second conversation described his interaction with students as "construction of a dialogue that is as objective as we can make it." And in our third conversation he described his "insistence on coherent discussions" as based in his "belief that the [learning] environment that we need to construct is one that has to have some objectivity." By the third iteration the vocabulary that Manny used to describe his image of himself as teacher, and his understanding of his students as learners, was a vocabulary that repeatedly referred to a metaphor that, following his own terminology, I characterized as "the construction of an objective dialogue" metaphor.

After I had completed my series of observations of each design studio teacher, and after having conducted and transcribed the series of conversations I had with each of them, I began to analyze their narratives for the embedded theoretical content that supported their understanding of themselves as teachers, and of their students as learners. Metaphor played an important role in my approach to analyzing the relationship between theories of knowledge and teaching practices within each of the three study participants' narratives. The metaphors that each of the three participants invented as they rendered their verbal portraits of themselves and of their students pointed toward the set of descriptive definitions of their students' ways of knowing. These descriptive definitions included what knowledge students had or did not have about designing before their first studio experiences, how a student's knowledge of designing was acquired or made, the levels of knowledge that their students exhibited, the validity of some students' higher levels of knowledge as compared to other students' lower levels, the role of a student's subjective knowledge of themselves *as compared to* their objective knowledge of their work, the role of knowledge within a student's logic and reasoning processes, the role of knowledge within a student's intuitive processes, the knowledge capacities that students had or lacked, and the relation between knowledge and a student's capacity for verbally articulating his or her ideas.

I will discuss the implications of these teachers' various metaphors in terms of the modern literary conception of *metaphoric impermanence* in the concluding chapter. Now I want to introduce you to the three teachers whose theory and practice narratives I will explore fully in the chapters that follow. Emerson "Manny" Bradley (who you have been partially introduced to above) was in his early thirties, and received his undergraduate degree in architecture from Rice University. He graduated from Columbia University with a Masters Degree in Architecture. He employed two of his former students and two others in his small Oakland practice. His was a licensed architect in California as well as Texas. He began working for one of San Francisco's larger architecture firms in 1988, and four years later he struck out on his own and steadily built up his own architectural practice.

Joe Constantino, in his early forties, was both a graduate student and undergraduate student at the UCLA School of Architecture. After graduating with masters degrees in 1979, he and a classmate started their own practice in Los Angeles. In 1989, after their partnership dissolved, Joe moved to San Francisco, where he worked independently as a one-person architectural practice. Gina Vismara, in her mid thirties, was born and grew up in Rome, Italy. She immigrated to the United States and entered Berkeley's Department of Architecture as an undergraduate in 1981. She received her Masters Degree in Architecture from Yale University in 1990. Gina, like Joe, practiced as a one person architectural office. She, her husband, and three year old son resided in Richmond, California, in a neighborhood that is known for its ethnic diversity.

In upcoming chapters, Manny's, Joe's, and Gina's voices and vocabularies for speaking about themselves and about their beginning design studio students will be presented. Within these chapters I used their voices and their vocabularies to render portraits of the theoretical places that housed their sets of teaching practices. My descriptions were meant to evoke your resonance with, or dissonance in response to, each of these teacher's voices and vocabularies. Empathy with or reaction against any of the upcoming descriptions of various teaching approaches was intended to enable you to compare your approach to learning relationships with the approaches described here. I believe that understanding one's own teaching practice approaches relative to those of one's colleagues, who might hold unfamiliar sets of educational ideas and approaches, is a first step in a process of working collaboratively toward a fuller understanding of existing teaching practices, as well as working toward the formulation of new practices to be tested in the future.

Chapter Four

Manny: The Territory of Objectivity

The Invisible Image of the Teacher

UC Berkeley's Department of Architecture is housed in Wurster Hall, a large, modern, U-shaped structure whose main feature is a formidable concrete tower whose balconies face directly west. The ninth floor balcony of the tower enjoys a local reputation among architecture students for being the best spot on the Berkeley campus to catch a picture postcard view of the university surroundings, and beyond that the San Francisco Bay, and beyond that the skyline of San Francisco, the Golden Gate Bridge, and the Pacific Ocean meeting the California sky at the horizon. I often anticipated the view as I rode the elevator up to the ninth floor, where I observed architect Manny Bradley teaching his beginning design studio.

On one particular morning as I stepped out of the elevator I spotted a student standing alone on the ninth floor balcony. He was apparently enjoying the view. His back was turned toward me as he faced away from the elevator lobby toward the view. He had on a pair of headphones, and his head moved from side to side to the rhythms coming from the small Walkman clipped to his belt. He didn't hear me approaching because the music that permeated his ears was at a high volume that kept other sounds from penetrating his consciousness. But when I pulled the sliding glass door back to enter the balcony he turned toward me, took off his headset, smiled, and asked me why I was always coming up to the ninth floor. When he turned I recognized him. Jonathan was an undergraduate junior in his early twenties. He was not in Manny's section, but in another architect's section in the same studio that Manny officially led. The studio, as a whole, was comprised of five sections. Each section of fifteen students was led by one teacher. Manny was the leader of the entire group of teachers (or as they were called, "studio critics").

I explained to Jonathan that I was studying the teaching and learning of design and that my visits comprised the "field observation" phase of my investigation. Within our conversation Jonathan told me that he was not having a good semester (which was half over by then) because he and his teacher "didn't get along very well." He told me when the semester began his first choice for a teacher, "by far," was Manny. When I asked him about his preference he told me that *his* studio critic was "too soft" and that from what he had heard Manny was not afraid to "punch hard" when it came to criticizing student work. Jonathan formed his right hand into a fist and, imitating a prizefighter, he swung it through the air as he told me "I can take a verbal punch. Some people don't like Manny. We heard he got in trouble for some of the things he did last year. We heard that down in the lobby he made this one girl cry about what he was telling her about her project. I think it's great. He's direct, I like that better."

When I asked Jonathan what he felt and perceived the difference was between *his* studio critic and Manny, he told me that "My critic goes on and on for an hour and repeats what he says, and doesn't get to the point. In the lobby last semester I saw Manny take a column from one of the model buildings that a student had built and use it as a toothpick. " Jonathan laughed and continued, "I thought that was great. I tried getting into his section, but I didn't get in. I don't think it's good to stroke and be so gentle with students. To say, 'Oh that's good. Everything is going to be O.K. You'll graduate and leave and make a million dollars.' A lot of them have grown up spoiled. I did not grow up that way."

The vocabulary that Jonathan chose to narrate the story of his "self" in many ways interlocked with his vocabulary for talking about his teachers. Within his narrative Jonathan portrayed himself as the opposite of the student who was spoiled by a "gentle, stroke giving" teacher. Unlike the "spoiled" students, Jonathan was able, indeed willing and wanting, to "take a verbal punch" from his teacher. His willingness to endure the pain that his teacher administered was proof that unlike some of his spoiled classmates he had what it took to be a real architect in a professional world of harsh realities and limited monetary compensation.

For Jonathan, Manny was the kind of teacher who could meta-phorically beat him into shape. Manny, in Jonathan's narrative of his "self," was a hard "puncher," a teacher who "told his students what to do." Who literally used student models for toothpicks, and who sometimes "made them cry" in the process. A teacher whose words stung, and whose actions (like using part of a student's model as a toothpick) were powerful and controlling, supported Jonathan's view of himself as tough and unspoiled.

Jonathan's language for describing his preferred relationship with a teacher in terms of being a "student who took the teacher's verbal punches" marked his use of traditional vocabulary that supported the idea that the student's relation to the teacher was based on inequality and separation. In the relationship between student and teacher, where the student "took" the teacher's "verbal punches," the student was seen as a passive receiver of something that both participants implicitly (or explicitly) agreed would benefit the receiver. The student's vocabulary was part of the system in which one participant was an active conveyor of punches and the other was a passive recipient. Rather than a "give and take" between the teacher's verbal capacities (their language) and the student's, the teacher did all the giving and the student all the taking.

Jonathan's representation of Manny pointed to his (Jonathan's) own conception of the student-teacher relationship. Within Jonathan's metaphor, surviving an apprenticeship with a tough-minded, tough-sounding teacher, was his way of proving his early-twenties self to the world. Jonathan's narrative of self was a reminder that students brought with them (to their first series of design studios) an archetypal image of the "Teacher": an image of how teachers act, speak, and treat their students. The invisible archetype that students carried of the Teacher was brought to bear upon the teacher's own conception of who they were as educators. Students' preconceived images of the types of actions that their teacher was likely to take, the teachers' possible repertoire of gestures toward them, the tone of their voice, and the vocabulary they spoke were all parts of the archetypal set of expectations that they brought onto the stage where teaching and learning were enacted.[1]

Their invisible image of the Teacher was at the same time a way of expressing the self that students constructed through their interaction with their teachers. In Jonathan's case, his expectations of what Manny *might be like* as his teacher emerged through the vocabulary that he constructed as he and I spoke. Jonathan's "I can take a verbal punch" metaphor embodied the traditional educational thesis that the student's relationship with the teacher grew around the fact that the teacher's higher knowledge was a more powerful, more legitimate form of knowledge, as compared to the student's lower form. Within the traditional vocabulary, the teachers, because they possessed higher, intrinsic knowledge, were endowed with the license to demand that the language that the students needed to learn, if they were to learn at all, was the teacher's language.

Constructing an Objective Dialogue

At various points in our series of conversations about the process of design education, Manny posed himself as an alternative to the teacher who thought that learning amounted to the student learning the teacher's language. "I think that there is much too much in their previous experience," he told me, "that is about relying upon a teacher to tell them what's right and what's good; a whole educational system's worth. And suddenly they've got somebody saying that they actually have to participate in decisions. That they have to evaluate and come down on one side of the discussion, or another, for themselves. They can't just count on the teacher saying, 'Do this, this is good, this is right, move that, push this over here, put a door there,' which I don't do and I won't do."

Manny spoke of his interest in developing a model of teaching that resulted in students defining their own "propositions" that, in turn, would become the rationale for solving the kinds of design problems they would ultimately have to face as architects. He spoke of his model for teaching in comparison to models where the students "emulated" the teacher, rather than developing their own propositions and intentions. "There's this kind of teaching that you see in architecture schools too often where it's about emulating rather than learning," he reflected, "and I think that it codifies these hierarchical structures. You know: I am the one to be emulated, you are the one to emulate. I try very hard to deconstruct that kind of hierarchy in the studio."

His students' language, as well as his own, emerged as one of Manny's central concerns as he and I talked about his way of teaching, and about his students' ways of learning to design, and his attempt to "deconstruct the studio hierarchy" in which students emulated rather than learned. "Much of the teaching I attempt to do," Manny told me in one of our recorded conversations, "starts with the proposition that we are going to construct a dialogue that is as objective as we can make it. That we are going to work very hard to get outside of *I want, I like*." For Manny, the process in which the teacher and student engaged in the "construction of an objective dialogue" depended on an objective methodology in which the subjective point of view (in the form of the word "*I*") was censored from both the student's *and* the teacher's vocabulary.

Several of the fourteen students in Manny's studio section described Manny's insistence that they talk about their work without using the phrase "*I want*" or "*I like*" as "Manny's rule." Manny explained that he developed the "*no using I want, I like*" rule in an attempt to have students clearly define the intentions behind their work, and "to argue convincingly for them" without relying on their "self-indulgent" habits of speaking about their designs in the first person. Manny's rationale for the prohibition of the phrases "I want" and "I like" within his students' vocabularies interlocked with his belief that his students' "capacity to think, and to reason, and to argue and persuade were signs of the intelligence of educated beings." He believed that "clear thinking was manifest in clear speaking and the inability to speak clearly most often represented an inability to think clearly."

Manny associated clear thinking with mental abilities like reasoning, verbal articulation, and argumentation. He told me he believed that there was "much too much subjectivity" in the studios that other design teachers taught. He questioned whether learning could take place outside of learning aimed at arriving at objective, rather than subjective, conclusions to design problems. For a student to speak about design work in the first person "I" was a sign of "self-indulgent" behavior "driven by ego and identity," not by a search for what had historically been defined as "good architecture."

Manny's Standards

By Manny's standards of reasoning *and* his ability to think and speak clearly, Sam was his best student, "a joy" as Manny characterized him at one point in our conversations. He spoke about Sam, telling me, "I think Sam inevitably gets the framework of what I say. Sam thinks very clearly. You can reason well with Sam. And he always understands the line of thought that I use in critiquing his work." But at the beginning of the semester Sam was not "a joy," in that he (Sam) relied on the kind of "self-indulgent" habits that Manny perceived as detrimental to learning. Manny explained, "Sam initially reacted to everything I said with a counterargument. And it was just because I think he wanted to be perceived as somebody who had an intellect or whatever. And I came up to him privately one day and I said to him, 'Sam I just want to let you know that there is a kind of way of interacting that's taking place here that is actually counter-productive to your learning. And here is what it is: as soon as I say something you are immediately countering it rather than hearing it, thinking about it.' "

Emphasizing that reasoning rather than reacting was what he expected of his students, Manny told Sam, "I'd feel much better if you came back to me an hour later and countered it because you had actually considered it enough to decide how valid the comment was, relative to what you have been working on." As he reflected on Sam's response, Manny continued, "And I think he actually heard that and took it to heart and saw that it was impacting his learning and he is now probably in many ways much more open to criticism and in many ways he is accelerating his own education because of that. So it's been a kind of interesting reversal. I think the more confident a student is, the more capable they are of receiving criticism. I'm not talking about criticism like 'you're bad, this is no good,' that kind of thing, but 'well here's a place where your thinking got a little fuzzier, here's a place where it needs to get sharper.' Some students hear that and some students don't."

Manny's message to Sam was that learning was based on a process in which students needed to allow time for the valuable information that the teacher had transmitted to them to be processed through their reasoning and thinking faculties. When the students were in a reactive mode, when they spontaneously and unthinkingly responded to what the teacher was trying to convey to them, when they relied on the "ego" or their "identity" rather than their intellectual capacity to reason, the result was "counterproductive to learning."

Flora: Forced to Think

Flora, one of five women in their early twenties in his section, was an example of a student that Manny considered problematic because of her inability to think and respond to a problem based on his "preferred model" of learning by objective reasoning. Toward the end of the semester Flora, as well as the other students in Manny's section, had been assigned the design of an overnight hostel located in an industrial area of San Francisco, adjacent to the downtown business, shopping, and cultural district. At the far end of the ninth floor studio, inside of a small free-standing four-walled structure (that was referred to as "the cube"), Manny met with Flora and three of her classmates to review their preliminary plans for the hostel. Flora's approach to her design, as she explained it, started with her finding existing buildings in the area that she liked. She then photographed the buildings she liked and picked out certain elements (like doors, windows, facade materials, colors) from those buildings that she thought she could use in her own design to make her new building "fit in" with the others.

Manny's response to her work centered around the criticism that she had not developed any argument for why the buildings that she liked were "good." As a result her statement that her design was a response to the existing context was not being backed up by convincing evidence that the buildings that she had chosen as architectural exemplars embodied those qualities that made exemplary architecture. Midway through her presentation, Manny pointed to the flaw in her logic, by telling Flora, "If you say that 'I want to respond to what's here,' then you must argue that what's here is good. You can't just say this building sucks and so mine is going to do the same." Flora and the other three students in "the cube" turned their eyes toward Manny. He tilted his chair back slightly, balancing himself on the back legs of the chair.

Flora responded, "Can I continue even if you don't like my building?"

Manny tilted forward again and as the two front legs of the chair clicked onto the concrete floor he told Flora, "It is incumbent to argue for what you are doing. Not just here in an academic setting but with a client, or a review board, or a city council." He paused for a second or two, and as he did he spotted a razor-sharp Exacto blade on the tabletop and he reached over to pick it up. He continued, "you must convince those who also participate in this process. And convincing requires the ability to argue persuasively for those visions you hold." As he spoke he held the small blade between his thumb and index finger. Then he shifted it from his right to left hand and held it so that the sharp tip pressed slightly into his index finger and the dull end balanced in the center of his thumb. "If the argument is that your building should fit into the context with the others," he spoke slowly and deliberately, "then why would you replicate those others without saying why the others are good or bad? You are not going to be convincing unless you can stand up and say why you draw on certain buildings and why they work."

Manny then put the Exacto blade back onto the table and commented that the Marriott Hotel (which was one of the buildings that Flora liked) was ugly. Flora quickly responded, "What makes *it* ugly?" Her voice climbed in pitch steadily until she reached the word "it," which she accented dramatically. Later that week when Manny and I spoke about this particular design critique session he told me, "The kind of question that Flora asked, 'Why is this ugly?' was intimidating as hell to an instructor." I told Manny that I was surprised: that he didn't seem intimidated at all. He responded saying, "Well I probably don't give away too much one way or another. I think those are words we use cavalierly without being prepared to actually articulate what it means when a student says, 'Why is that ugly?' or 'Why is this a good building?' or 'Why is this a bad building?' If you haven't really thought about it, it's a question that can really catch you off guard."

Manny's intimidation at being asked a question by a student that he had no ready answer for pointed to his belief that "clear thinking was manifest in clear speaking," and that clear thinking was a result of deliberating on a question, or an issue, or in this case on a feeling that "the Marriott was ugly." In the interchange with Flora, Manny had reacted spontaneously to the Marriott. That is, he had not deliberated on the reasons that his conclusion that "the Marriott is ugly" was a valid conclusion. The statement "the Marriott is ugly" was the kind of subjective statement that he considered more in the context of "ego" and "identity" than in reason, or logical analysis, or objectivity. It was the kind of statement that the invention of "Manny's Rule" was meant to exempt from the "construction of an objective dialogue." A dialogue that remained within the territory of the context of ideas, reason, and thought, and purposely did not cross into the territory of the subjective, the emotional, the spontaneous, the uninformed.

Manny's momentary lapse into the territory of the subjective was a rare event because he was very conscious that his model of teaching purposely disallowed such lapses in an attempt to keep the dialogue between his students and himself within the context of ideas and reason. Two thirds into the semester I asked Manny whether or not he thought that Flora was "getting it." That is, was Flora benefiting from his approach to teaching design. He told me, "Flora is somebody who really for the first time in her life is being forced to think about architecture in the context of ideas. In the context of the intellect. And I think it's an area where she is decidedly uncomfortable and very poorly trained to think and talk about her work in those terms. I have had similar students who come into the program very unprepared for the level of thought that I expect or put out as a preferred model. And no, she's not particularly getting it. And in honesty I think she probably won't."

As opposed to Sam, who *had* gotten "the framework" of Manny's "objective dialogue" approach, and who "always understood the line of thought" used in critiquing his (Sam's) work, Flora did not have those characteristics (the capacity to think, reason, argue, and persuade) that Manny defined as "signs of the intelligence of educated beings." For Manny those capacities were of a higher order than the ones she possessed. Manny further elaborated on his belief that Flora could not rise above the lesser level of "technical competence," into the level of "reason and intellect," telling me, "She is not a student who I am concerned about at the level of just kind of rote, technical competence. She can draw, she can make a plan, she can draw an elevation, she can organize buildings as long as the organization is relatively straightforward, all the rooms have light, all the circulation works. She has addressed all the kind of dumb stuff. So I don't worry about her ability in that sense. What I worry about is her poetic capacities. So I'm more than happy to not press her on *the demonstrate to me that you can organize a building,* and push her or give her more time or make the focus of her study for the remainder of the semester one that's more about: learn what it means to have a premise for your work. To have a proposition that underlies what you do."

Kristin: She Doesn't Believe

Manny considered four students out of the fourteen in his studio section as problematic. Three of the four problematic students were women. Flora's problem, as Manny described it, was her inability to "think of architecture in the context of ideas." Kristin, another of the three problematic women in his section, suffered from the inability to suspend her disbelief in the things that Manny proposed as essential in learning to design. Manny characterized Kristin as problematic because of her resistance to complying with the basic tenets that lay at the heart of his pedagogical approach to the learning of design. One of Manny's basic learning tenets that Kristin resisted was the "implicit belief" in architecture as a discipline.

"She doesn't believe," Manny told me, "and she doesn't believe just because she doesn't want to believe. There is a kind of student that you get at Berkeley. They come in and for some reason they decide to study architecture but with the already formulated belief that the study of architecture is elitist. That somehow the things we talk about, the things we focus on are of relevance only to us architects and they don't have anything to do with how people experience architecture in the world. And Kristin is kind of along that line, somehow. She doesn't have any implicit belief in the fact that it's a discipline that you have to study and learn. And believes that it's a kind of self-perpetuating myth. And I don't know what to say to a person like that to convince them otherwise."

For Manny, Kristin came into the beginning design studio with preconceived notions about architecture that deterred her from understanding that architecture was "a discipline" that required rigorous study to be mastered. Manny recognized that "society as a whole had empowered or entrusted architects with building the world that we all inhabited." The "implicit belief" in the discipline of architecture was an essential starting point toward learning what Manny described as the "ennobled qualities" of architecture. The huge responsibility that society had put upon the architect could not be taken lightly, and entrance into the profession required that students had an "implicit belief" in the "ennobled qualities" that made architecture a discipline in the first place.

A student like Kristin, who believed in the notion that architecture was "elitist" and that architects did not design in response to ordinary people, reflected the kind of disbelief in what was known to be implicitly true to her teachers. As he spoke to me about Kristin, in particular, Manny said, "She doesn't impress me as someone who has a lot of faith in what the better aspects of architecture are. And I just struggle with why somebody who has that opinion is studying architecture. A lot of times her attitude, I could sum it up, she hasn't actually said this, but I can sum it up very simply by the fact that she sits there thinking, 'This is all bullshit. Why are we talking about this stuff? This doesn't matter.' " For Manny, Kristin and others like her were frustrating because they often could not be convinced of what architecture was really all about. They were seemingly blind to "the better aspects of architecture," and that blindness led them to an unwarranted attitude that made Manny wonder why they would choose to study architecture at all.

During the urban hostel project, Kristin was exploring the use of large round staircases to accent the corners of her building. When I talked to her about Manny's response to her design she told me that he wondered why she had chosen a round shape, rather than a rectangular shape, for her staircases. She said that Manny wanted her to "state the intention behind her round staircases" and that she was "not very skillful" at stating things "the way Manny wanted." Kristin perceived her lack of skill as a matter of not understanding Manny's language for talking about design: that Manny's language sounded as if he was talking to his colleagues, not to students who were unfamiliar with the vocabulary that architects spoke. Hours after she talked to Manny about her round stairs, Kristin changed them from round to square.

Manny told me he felt frustrated by students like Kristin, who "ultimately went along with a design because their teacher was telling them they should. Not because they necessarily had an implicit belief that what their teacher was professing was useful." The "profound level" of frustration that Manny felt about Kristin's lack of implicit belief in the usefulness of the objective methodology that he professed was evoked by her resistance to designing based on a set of objective rather than subjective criteria. He perceived her defense of her round stairs as an opinion based on personal preference, rather than a clearly articulated proposition based on a well reasoned objective argument.

Manny described Kristin's insistence on remaining in the territory of the subjective as "a difficult perspective to confront" given that it opposed his own "objective" approach. As he put it, "The teaching I attempt to do starts with the proposition that we are going to construct a dialogue that is as objective as we can make it. That we are going to work very hard to get outside of 'I want, I like.' With Kristin I just don't think she's gotten beyond the belief that it's really just one person's opinion versus another's, that my opinion is as good as yours, and yours is as good as theirs."

Problem Students and Poetic Capacities

Manny's belief that his students needed to "get beyond" the belief that "good architecture" was based on personal opinion (or that everyone's opinion was equivalent in status) marked his use of a traditional educational vocabulary that started with the premise that knowledge existed at a higher level, as compared to opinion, personal preference, or subjective feeling. Manny's "construction of an objective dialogue" was one variation of a traditional vocabulary in which personal opinions were not candidates for entry into a higher level of knowledge and "human intelligence." Confirmation that the student had reached a higher level of knowledge required that students clearly articulated, through words, that they had the capacity to think, to reason, to dispassionately argue for their "propositions." A student like Kristin, whose impulse toward round shapes was uninformed by anything outside of her personal interests, may not have had the capacities of intelligence that Manny considered fundamental to the learning of design.

For speakers of the traditional educational vocabulary like Manny, opinion could never have the status of knowledge acquired through an objective methodology. He purposely developed "Manny's Rule," which censored the use of the "I want" and "I like" language from his students' vocabularies, because he believed that the construction of an "objective dialogue" was a viable pedagogical method for weaning students from their previous self-indulgent habits of confusing subjective opinion with objective knowledge. Manny's thesis that a higher level of knowledge was revealed through students' capacity for clear verbal articulation of their thoughts interlocked with his thesis that certain words indicated a higher level of objective reasoning while other words indicated a lower level of "ego" and "self-indulgence." The lower-level words (or thoughts, or opinions), for Manny, because they smacked of subjectivity, had no place in a dialogue that sought evaluation of problems through reason and objectivity.

The traditional educational vocabulary that supported the thesis that "right and good" existed beyond what the student personally believed was right or good, interlocked with the thesis that there was an intrinsic difference between teacher and student. Within the traditional vocabulary for talking about teaching and learning, an official external entity of some sort was required to legitimize what counted or did not count as knowledge because that vocabulary was driven by the idea that personal interest and experience were qualities of a lesser level of knowing that could never be counted as official knowledge. Although Manny did not want to think of himself as following in the footsteps of the traditional teacher (that his students were used to) who told his students "Do this, this is good, this is right," he nevertheless traveled down an educational path well trodden by a vocabulary based on separate kinds of knowledge and the need for an external force to weed out the lower forms of opinion and subjectivity from a higher kind of objectivity.

Manny went only half way in breaking from the tradition that required that students rely on their teacher to tell them what was right or good because he substituted the students' dependency on their teacher to tell them what was right or good with the students' dependency on an objectifying methodology. Whether the student depended on the teacher to know what was right or good, or whether the student depended on an objective method to know what was right or good, the assumption that underlay either was that a source outside of subjective experience was required if what was really right or really good was to be genuinely known. Within the model of teaching and learning that Manny enacted, the teacher controlled the vocabulary, the modes of thinking, and the self-expressions that were allowed entry into the "objective dialogue."

In Manny's narrative of teaching and learning design, the good student was one that made the reversal from talking about the work in the first person voice of the "I" to talking about the work in objective language based on historical precedent and an "implicit belief" in the "ennobled qualities of architecture." The problematic students, most of whom were women, were those who resisted talking about their work as if their experience of the work was based

on anything outside of their experience of their work. Manny's vocabulary for defining the "signs of intelligence of educated human
beings" followed in the long tradition of assuming that talk about
intelligence was talk about the mind and the mind's facility for
reason, calculation, objectivity, and the generation of precise words
that corresponded to precise intentions.

Manny termed Flora's ability to develop, organize, and plan
rooms and building circulation as competence in the "dumb stuff" of
design, as opposed to an ability to think of architecture in the context
of ideas, which he termed "poetic capacities." Within the traditional
Platonic conception of the poet's capacities, words were used to
discover an objective and universal essence about the world and its
objects. Following in Plato's footsteps, educators through the
centuries have believed that the capacities of the mind, like the poet's
capacity with words, were aimed at discovering what was true, and
right, and good about the world. Manny's interest in students'
developing a set of "poetic capacities" followed the Platonic
tradition that truth was inherent within language. 2

"Poetic capacity" in the traditional sense assumed, as Manny
assumed, that words could precisely reflect what was known about
the world: that words spoken could mirror, or correspond to, an
objective truth that existed outside of the subjective self. And that in
order to speak those words that truly reflected the objective state of
a building, or a neighborhood, or a city, the speakers had to find
some method, or some way of speaking about those things outside of
themselves that was not tainted by what they liked, or what they
wanted, or what they felt. "Poetic capacity," in Manny's usage,
implied that what was spoken aimed at the "construction of an
objective dialogue." Put another way, "poetic capacity" was
capacity to view the world through the objective machinery of the
mind; to use the mind to filter out subjective bias. The objectifying
machinery of the mind allowed for the processing of external
information through reason and logic. An "objective dialogue" gave
the mind the kind of input it needed to think of words that exactly
expressed what one had found to be "right" or "good." How clearly
his students' spoken *words* came to precisely reflecting *thoughts*
determined the extent of, or the lack of, their "poetic capacity."

On a Certain Blindness

The architect's language, for Manny, was by necessity a language
supported by the force of reason: a force that Manny believed could

ultimately persuade the client of the architect's "intentions." Emphasizing the client's control of the building design and construction enterprise, Manny told me, "I don't operate in the world, and I think the vast majority of architects don't operate in the world, where we are afforded the luxury of saying *"I want, I like."* Because ultimately what a client wants, what a client likes, will carry the day every time." Because the client's, rather than the architect's, subjective likes and dislikes "carried the day every time," Manny believed it made little sense for the architect to defend a design on personal grounds. Rather, the higher ground of reason and logic posed through an objective vocabulary was the only viable alternative when it came to defending one's architectural work.

The architect's language, for Kristin, was one that was foreign to her ears. Kristin told me that in one of her conversations with Manny she told him she did not understand a lot of what he was saying. The way Kristin put it to Manny was that since she "wasn't his colleague" that "he had to simplify" what he was telling her. Manny did not think it a problem that his students misunderstood him because they were unfamiliar with the language he used in conversation with them. He told me that he purposely "made a point of constructing a dialogue" that his students would not understand because he hoped that would force them into asking questions about the language he used. The problem as Manny described it was that students rarely asked that kind of question. Manny believed that problematic students like Kristin and Flora failed to speak the architect's language because they lacked the intellect and "poetic capacity" required to "construct an objective dialogue," or they blindly refused to adopt an "implicit belief" in the architect's "noble" mission and in "the better aspects of architecture."

I think that William James's essay "On a Certain Blindness in Human Beings," in his *Talks to Teachers,* can lend some perspective to a situation that often occurs in learning relationships where teachers believe that their students just don't understand, or just can't understand, what the teacher knew to be the right approach, or the best way, or the inherent truth. Writing in Cambridge, Massachusetts, in 1892, describing a trip he took through the rural environment of the southern states, James wrote:

> Some time ago, while journeying in the mountains of North Carolina, I passed a large number of 'coves,' as they call them there, or heads of small valleys between the hills, which had been newly cleared and planted. The impression on my mind was one of unmitigated squalor. The settler in every case cut down the more manageable trees, and left

their charred stumps standing... The forest had been destroyed; and what had 'improved' it out of existence was hideous, a sort of ulcer, without a single element of artificial grace to make up for the loss of Nature's beauty... I said to the mountaineer who was driving me, "What sort of people are they who have to make these new clearings?" "All of us," he replied. "Why, we ain't happy here, unless we are getting one of these coves under cultivation." I instantly felt that I had been losing the whole inward significance of the situation. Because to me the clearings spoke naught but denudation. I thought that to those whose sturdy arms and obedient axes had made them they could tell no other story. But, when they looked onto the hideous stumps, what they thought of was personal victory. The chips, the girdled trees, and the vile split rails spoke of honest sweat, persistent toil and final reward... In short, the clearing, which to me was a mere ugly picture on the retina, was to them a symbol redolent with moral memories and sang a very pœan of duty, struggle, and success. I had been blind to the peculiar ideality of their conditions as they certainly would have been to the ideality of mine, had they had a peep at my strange indoor academic ways of life at Cambridge.[3]

James's message, as he wrote elsewhere in the same essay, was that, "The subject judged knows a part of the world of reality which the judging spectator fails to see."[4] The "judging spectator" suffers from a "certain blindness" when his or her eyes take in the picture of the "subject judged" without considering the story that the "subject judged" had to tell and the metaphors that they had constructed to tell *their* story. His first assumption about the inhabitants of the forest environment that he was experiencing was that they "could tell no story" about Nature different from his own. James's "story" about rural environments, which he constructed prior to his visit, was built upon a set of interlocking metaphors that pointed to "Nature's beauty": metaphors supportive of the kinds of manipulations of nature that result in "artificial grace," not in an "ulcer" that ate away at nature's beauty.

At first, the descriptions that James created to make sense of his experience of a forest that had been partially clear-cut remained within his own "Nature's beauty" vocabulary: nature had been wronged, "the forest had been destroyed" and "denuded." But his "Nature's beauty" metaphor began to collapse when one of the native inhabitants spoke an entirely different story, constructed a new metaphor, that James had not previously considered. Within his native tour guide's vocabulary, the "clearings" equated to "cultivation," not "denudation." The singularity of James's own "judging spectator" vocabulary began collapsing as it entered the territory of language and metaphor created by the "subject judged."

As he experienced the collision between his own vocabulary, in which felled trees equated to "hideous stumps" *and* his driver's metaphors, in which felled trees equated to "personal victory," James realized that he "had been losing the whole inward significance of the situation." That is, he realized that as long as his pair of eyes saw the forest exclusively through the vocabulary that he had brought along with him, he would lose sight of what those who lived within the situation found significant about it. The "inward significance of the situation" emerged as James engaged in conversation with his guide. As the guide spoke, James heard a vocabulary, a set of words, phrases, and metaphors that signified an alternative conception of the same landscape that both he and his guide had experienced.

In the end James came to recognize *both* his own and the native inhabitants' narratives as legitimate descriptions of the same objective reality. James did not resist the idea that there could be many ways to describe the world, or that there could be many truths that could explain one world. James constructed a useful framework for understanding our relationship between our selves and our students in terms of the set of descriptions that both we as the "judging spectator" and they as the "subject judged" bring into a mutually experienced environment. His message was that teaching began with acknowledging the learner's vocabulary, set of metaphors, and methods of creating descriptions of selves and the world.

The vocabulary that Manny used to define the relationship between teacher and students signaled a certain pedagogical blindness to "the whole inward significance" of his students' situation: their way of seeing and describing the world as they saw it through their set of eyes, heard it through their pair of ears, and spoke it through their particular voices. Through the vocabulary that Manny brought into the landscape in which he interacted with Flora and Kristin he saw them as having less capacity, and less intelligence, and less implicit belief in architecture. Absent from Manny's "objective dialogue" with Flora was any talk about how Flora, herself, experienced the Marriott, or what mode of intelligence she used to formulate her opinion about it, or what kinds of tools (like photography) she used to represent it, or what the photographic form of representation had to do with the way she understood the Marriott. Absent from Manny's "objective dialogue" with Kristin was any talk about what in her past experience led to her interest in circular forms, or what she was trying to express by the use of a circular rather than a rectangular geometry, or whether

her modes of thinking were based on an interest in primarily emphasizing the use of a visual intelligence mode as opposed to using (at least in the case of the particular problem that confronted her) a logical, or a verbal mode of intelligence.[5]

Manny's narrative portrayals of Kristin and Flora marked his reliance on a traditional set of metaphors for describing the relationship between teacher and student. His exclusion of their wants and likes from the pedagogical method that he used to judge them, and his other students, rendered invisible his students' inner lives, their vocabulary for defining themselves, and their individual voices. At the same time Manny, himself, remained invisible to his students. As he put it, "I probably don't give away too much one way or another," meaning that he did not convey who he, was outside of his professional persona, to his students. And as a corollary to his belief that excluding his identity from the process of teaching was a way of objectifying the conversation with his student, his students' selves were also excluded from the conversation.

Kristin and Flora's resistance to Manny's singular option for constructing the objective dialogue between teacher and student raised the question, "Who is to say what counts and does not count as a legitimate language, a legitimate vocabulary, a legitimate metaphor for describing knowledge of the world to one's self or to others?"[6] What Manny heard in Flora's and Kristin's voices was that they lacked capacity in the areas of reason, idea, and objectivity. But perhaps Flora's and Kristin's voices echoed a conception of teaching and learning that William James voiced over a century ago: that particular people thought and communicated in particular ways; that to assume that there was one standard for intelligence was to overlook the various intelligences through which various people expressed who they were in the world; that to assume that talking about one's work as if it was created outside of one's wants or one's needs was to overlook the intimacy between the thing created and its creator (or in certain cases the building designed and its designer); that to assume that the discrepancies between the student's language and the teacher's indicated a gap in the student's knowledge was to close one's eyes to the student's understanding of the world, to close one's ears to the metaphors in that student's vocabulary, and to close one's mind to the possibility that something could be learned from one's students.

Chapter Five

Joe: Listening for Their Vocabularies

A Varied Menu

As I rode the elevator from the Wurster Hall lobby up to architect Joe Constantino's sixth-floor studio over an eight-week observation period, I noticed that the architecture students who rode up with me very often carried with them some tool of the architectural trade. The equipment that students brought on the elevator with them included foot-long architect's scales, four-foot-long black plastic parallel bars, light green drafting board covers, various colors of "luxo" lamps, wooden-handled horse-hair drafting brushes, clear plastic triangles of various sizes, small black bound sketch books, colored pencils, mechanical pencils, pencil leads, lead pointers for sharpening their mechanical pencils, small metal erasing shields, "Exacto" matte knives, "Exacto" matte knife blades, semi-opaque white vellum drafting paper, gray chipboard, white foamcore board, brown corrugated cardboard, beige drafting tape, blue and white drafting dots, and most often a roll of yellow tracing paper. Once off the elevator, a turn to the immediate left brought into view a set of large black metal and glass doors. Beyond these doors was a large fifty-by-ninety-foot studio in which all the tools of the trade that students brought with them would eventually be used to make the models and produce the drawings that represented their design ideas.

A varied menu of activities occurred during the 1 to 6 p.m., three-day-a-week "studio time." The different activities that beginning design studio students engaged in reflected different aspects of the experiences that they were likely to encounter as practicing architects. During large group meetings the fifteen students in Joe's section joined the fifteen students in Karen Magruder's section to view slide photos that were pertinent to their assigned design problem: the design of buildings that would revitalize a three-block portion of Berkeley's downtown area. These large group meetings were a rehearsal for interchanges that architects had with community groups, city councils, or corporate clients.

In section meetings Joe's fifteen students often gathered around the large collaboratively built model of existing downtown Berkeley buildings. The large model consisted of chipboard buildings that represented an area near the downtown Berkeley BART subway stop. The larger model of downtown Berkeley buildings was constructed so that students could place their individual smaller models into the "context" of the existing buildings that surrounded their proposed building. Once a student's individual model was situated within the larger model, Joe and Karen would talk about the progress of that student's design. These section meetings rehearsed students for the critique sessions that were an everyday part of the dynamics within architectural practice. [1]

Right from the Gut

Within our conversations together, Joe consistently described his students' designs as outgrowths of the many "sides" that students brought to their studio work: their previous set of life experiences, their ideas, the vocabulary they used to describe their work, and the intuitions they felt within the process of designing. Within the first week of the eight-week design of a building in downtown Berkeley, students made use of their artistic "sides" in a two-day "Three Dimensional Objects Exercise." In this first exercise, students built models (made of materials of their choice: wood, Styrofoam, chipboard, or clay) through which they explored the visual relationships between basic geometric forms (squares, circles, cubes, spheres, and cones). Within their second two-day exercise, a "Site Analysis of the Berkeley Downtown," students made use of their analytic "sides" by collecting and presenting the "hard data" that they gathered about buildings, history, traffic/pedestrian patterns, zoning requirements, geography, and environmental issues within their study area.

In the last three days of their first week, students made use of their "intuitive sides" by engaging in a "conceptual models" exercise in which each of them produced eight building models. Each of their models expressed how their particular building's geometric composition of shapes was determined by responding to the set of existing contextual conditions within the downtown Berkeley site (existing conditions, for example, might have included pedestrian areas, large or historic buildings, or places with interesting views). Joe's approach was to have his students make eight models within an amount of time so limited that completing the exercise on time would, in the end, depend on them learning to trust that their first, quickly felt intuitions, which even though vague or still not articulated in terms of their practicality or their realism, were expressive of an "overall" idea.

Elaborating on the emphasis on having students learn to trust their "intuitive, visceral responses," Joe told me that within his approach he was "trying to encourage an analysis of the problem in that kind of quick response as opposed to some sort of learned and step by step rational way to approach it." He emphasized that one of his aims in teaching young student designers was to have them understand the importance of finding ways to balance the intuitive with the rational, or as Joe put it, "to never lose track of one or the other. Because a lot of times students will begin a studio by doing something very intuitive, but they put it away when they start the rational process."

For Joe the quick, spontaneous, "animal response" was important because it validated his students' uniquely felt intuitions as a legitimate form of "analysis" within the design process. Joe recognized that young designers tended to lose touch with their intuitions, and he perceived this as problematic because he believed that the designers' "search for a coherent overall project expression" most often came early on in their exploration and could be felt, as he put it, "right from the gut." As designers, students would learn that trusting their spontaneous intuitions was an important part of the design process because the designer's first impressions about a site (or about any other aspect of the design) often became the initial basis for later development of an "overall idea" that would ultimately enable the various parts of the building to be perceived as a whole.

Joe recognized the importance of the "step-by-step, rational approach" within the design process, but he understood that his student's initial "visceral, animal" responses were often put aside and forgotten when they began dealing with the building's more practical aspects. As they arrived at the practical phase of the design process, students tended to shift into an entirely "rational" mode of exploration, rather than shifting into a search based on a balance between their rational and intuitive modes. He understood that within the seven upcoming weeks of designing, his students' modes of navigating through the design problem would quickly shift from first impressions, intuitions, and feelings to the "rational search" for a building structure, or to a realistic response to budgetary constraints. The fading out, or eventual disappearance, of their initial intuitive, gut-level responses to their designs was problematic because these feelings marked starting points within their search for an "overall expression."

Joe understood that much of designing was a trial and error process in which going back to an original set of starting points was essential if the designer was to regain his or her bearings after testing a particular idea that ultimately proved to be unfruitful. The sustenance of his students' "visceral" responses was important within this testing process because *if* their intuitive starting points could be held in readiness, even as they entered the "rational phase" of the process, *then* they (the intuitive starting points) could be immediately available whenever a student needed a marker to point him or her back to a previous direction after a journey down a back road led to a dead end.

When they reached the phase of the more "rational searches," their earlier, eight, quickly built models could become the markers that could point them to the next step in their search for a "coherent overall project expression." Their early models could serve to remind students of the instincts they followed and the personal motivations that emerged for them as they pursued their search for the "overall expression." The early models, in other words, could enable students to keep the end of the design process in view, even as they were still on the road and not yet at the end of their design journeys. Joe understood that without the personal motivation to drive their designs forward students were in danger of "floating free and detached, with no basis for pulling in the forms" that at journey's end would unify the building's complex set of aesthetic, social, and functional considerations.

Authoring and Owning Their Designs

The message that Joe wanted to get across to his students through the "eight conceptual models" exercise was, as he put it, "that they came up with that." That they "owned" not just one, but eight potential designs that emerged within a process in which their feelings and thoughts were being expressed through the architect's formal language of geometric shapes, volumes, and voids. Joe told me that he thought it was very important for students to have the sense of "authorship and owning" of their designs. His set of teaching practices were developed to help facilitate the student's sense that the designs they created were always an outgrowth of their own processes of creating them. The quick, three-day model making experiences that Joe took his students through were specifically intended to address the student's individually felt responses to the design problem of revitalizing Berkeley's downtown district.

Another one of Joe's approaches to having his students realize that they owned their design works in much the same way that authors own their written works was to have them verbalize as many of their ideas and feelings as they possibly could within a very short time. In individual conversations with his students, Joe often asked them to speak "Whatever came into their mind." I asked him about his method of giving students "five seconds" to describe what they were feeling and thinking at the early stage of their building designs. Joe told me, "Because they're shy they don't know what to say. So I tell them make a mistake, say something, say something else so you learn two things. One: you can say something that may be a mistake and keep going. By forcing yourself to challenge yourself to think about it differently you, yourself, can come up, within a minute or two, with five different ways of looking at it that you hadn't thought of the minute before. Secondly: it's O.K. to come up with something and say it's wrong. So you say, 'It didn't really work out.' You keep going until all of a sudden something starts to make sense to you and to the person you're working with. So I will do that a lot of times because a lot of people are just too shy to be wrong. They don't want to be wrong. When they say something they want it to be right. And sometimes there is no right. So you just say it. You just do it and you say it."

Joe's role in having his students speak their minds as a way of growing out of their "shyness about being wrong" was to listen to what his students were saying and to ask them to say more about it, or to repeat back to them, or paraphrase back to them, what they had told him. Reiterating his interest in his students' "authoring and owning their designs," Joe told me, "Sometimes I just keep rephrasing it and I want them to find it. I don't want me to find it. I want them to find it. And so all I do is I keep knocking at the door until they open."

Joe told me that when he was engaged in a "desk crit" with his students he tried to "clue into the student's wavelength." He began this "clueing in" process by asking them what they were trying to express, or where they were getting stuck. Three weeks into the seven-week project, I watched as Joe attempted to "clue into the wavelength" that would enable him to respond to a design that Roberto had developed. Roberto had chosen to design a cultural arts center as part of the revitalization plan for downtown Berkeley. Roberto told Joe that he was interested in exploring the relationship between the "planes" and "volumes" in his design.

The language of architectural building forms that Roberto had invented was one in which "theater spaces" were metaphorically likened to "volumes," and the hallways and exterior walls were metaphorically likened to geometric "planes." The eight "quick, intuitive response" models that he had constructed a few weeks earlier were on Roberto's desk. Joe picked up a small balsa wood model that Roberto had produced in the first week of the summer session. He brought it close to his own eyes to look for the intersection of volumes and planes that Roberto had described as his interest. Picking up Roberto's larger, more recent model, Joe told Roberto that the energy the small model conveyed had been lost in the translation to the larger scale model. That the smaller model expressed a much subtler interaction between planes and volumes, compared to the larger model where the volumetric shape of the theater had become as muscular as "Arnold Schwartzenegger."

In Roberto's larger most recent model the volume of the theater had become so large and obvious that it visually dominated the wall surfaces adjacent to it. Or put another way: the balance between the theater (as a volume) and the adjacent exterior walls (as a geometric plane) had been lost because the theater had become visually loud and overbearing. Joe conveyed his sense that somehow the dynamics that the more restrained earlier version possessed had been lost along the way. The new larger model, he told Roberto, had somehow become "static."

Putting down the smaller model, Joe began playing with pieces of the larger model as he and Roberto continued talking about possible directions that could be taken to recapture the energy of the previous model. Using what he calls his "more experienced eye," Joe manipulated certain sections of the model, tearing into the chipboard in order to remove sections of the exterior walls. The results of Joe's removing what he described as "the bulky, static volume of the main hallway" was that a huge opening in the exterior facade had been created. The opening, or "void" as Joe described it, was a dramatic counterpoint to the mass of the large volume of the theater above.

Ordinary and Unordinary Languages

Joe and I met at the Cafe Strada (a two-minute walk from Wurster Hall) to talk about his interaction with Roberto. He insisted that we leave Wurster Hall and go somewhere "completely different" so that he could unwind, relax, and reflect. The Cafe Strada, with its classical music in the background, its round outdoor tables, its warm cappuccino, and sweet pastries made Joe feel a comfortable distance from Wurster Hall. As he finished a bagel Joe reflected on the encounter with Roberto: "When I'm with a student we're co-designing is the way I see it. It's not me, it's not them, alone. It's us in conversation, going back and forth trying to figure it out and usually if we come up with something we've done it from their basis. Then we start exploring. So when they see it, and I see it, we both see it, it just feels right for both of us and we know it because we have shared the basis for it, which came from their thinking. And I got into it enough to where I could use *it* to find out where *they* were going."

Joe paused to pick up his cup of cappuccino, and carefully sipping it to make sure it had cooled down to a drinkable temperature, he told me, "I basically have to be ready. What's interesting about it, as an instructor, is that I go in and I just have to be loose enough. The challenge for me is to be on top of it enough so that with each student, I can sit there and figure it out, like a puzzle,[2] as we're talking about it. As they're talking, as I'm talking. And a lot of times I don't get into it. It's not something I see right away. Sometimes, a lot of times, we dig around, we talk, and then finally it starts coming to me. Once I see it, I see it. And that happened with Roberto. At first I didn't know why I didn't like his design. Why it wasn't working. But then after a while it made more and more sense what was going on and I think when I was finally able to explain it to him he just clicked."

At the beginning of their conversation Joe expressed his vague sense that he "did not like the design" when he told Roberto that it was "static." As their conversation moved forward, and Joe actually began manipulating Roberto's study model, Joe tried to find a way of talking about what he felt about Roberto's design in terms that originated in Roberto's vocabulary, rather than his (Joe's) own. Joe recalled the interaction with Roberto, telling me, "I moved the wall in one of his models, and that was important. When I shifted the volumes and moved the walls and looked at it, all of a sudden I realized that's why it had been so statically conceived. And even though it seemed to him dynamic, it couldn't have been more static. So then I had to figure out: O.K., understanding that, having done that, how could we go back to *his* original vocabulary on the pieces that were pretty successful and use *that* vocabulary to express this new understanding of what we just did?"

A critical assumption Joe made was that his students' "original vocabularies," which reflected their "ownership and authorship" of their creations, could become the basis for "figuring out" where their designs were headed. Based on that assumption Joe developed a listening and recording practice that enabled him to capture and feed back to his students their own ideas that, in his judgment, might fruitfully move their designs forward. As students talked about their designs, Joe wrote down certain phrases they verbalized that he believed were potentially useful in setting a direction for future exploration. In the early part of the forty-five-minute desk crit conversation, Joe wrote a series of phrases that Roberto used to describe the approach that he (Roberto) had taken in searching for an "overall form" for the building.

As Roberto spoke about his design search he used the phrase "there is no building" to describe those parts of his building façade that were similar to the voids in a modern sculpture. Roberto's "there is no building" phrase was one of several phrases that Joe took written notes on as Roberto verbalized his design ideas. At that time Joe could not have predicted that the "there is no building" phrase would be the one, among several phrases, that would be useful in furthering Roberto's design explorations. But as the conversation progressed, and especially after Joe and Roberto agreed that puncturing the huge (static) exterior wall was a way of regaining the dynamic tension between "volumes and planes" that was expressed in Roberto's early models, Joe realized that the "there is no building" phrase that Roberto had invented connected to Roberto's interest in experimenting with the use of voids in the building façade as a way expressing transparency. Voids in the building, in other words, could become architectural instances where "there was no building."

His listening and synthesizing abilities enabled Joe to connect Roberto's interest in "sculptural voids" and "transparency" with Roberto's "there is no building" phrase. The next step was to feed that phrase back to Roberto, who began to appreciate how the set of words he (Roberto) had spoken were expressive of the quality of transparency that he wanted his building to embody. This enabled Roberto to move forward, on his own, toward crystallizing that transparent quality in "built" form. Because Joe went back to an idea that Roberto had authored and owned, Roberto could continue to understand that "his ordinary spoken language" was a way of explaining to himself, and to others, what he was trying to express through the "unordinary architectural language" of building form and structure.

Poetic Process of Creation

Joe's descriptions of his set of teaching practices that were based on listening for the student's voice and vocabulary, in many ways implicated a nontraditional definition of knowledge *and* an unconventional set of premises about the interaction between teachers and students. The teacher in Joe's narrative of his interactions with his students was a teacher who listened for the emerging metaphors in his students' descriptions of their designs. The commitment to a set of teaching practices based on the premise that the teacher was expected to listen for the student's language reflected an abandonment of the teaching tradition in which the student must listen and learn to imitate the teacher's language because the teacher's form of language and knowledge was inherently separate, and of a higher kind, than the student's own.

The theory of knowledge that was implicated within Joe's narrative of his teaching practice of listening for the students' metaphorical descriptions of their work began with the recognition that felt intuitions, even though they were barely describable through spoken language, could eventually lead to the designer's formulation of their purpose, motivation, and ultimately their finding a "coherent overall project expression." Joe's interest in legitimizing his students' vague intuitions and the mistakes that they were likely to make as they invented different ways of talking about feelings (that could barely be talked about) echoed the process by which poets create poetry. Richard Rorty describes the poet's process, when writing:

> a poet...is typically unable to make clear exactly what it is he wants to do before developing the language in which he succeeds in doing it. His new vocabulary makes possible, for the first time, a formulation of its own purpose. It is a tool for doing something which could not have been envisaged prior to the development of a particular set of descriptions, those which it itself helps to provide.[3]

Joe's understanding of the poetic process of creation, in which his students were unable to explicitly define what it was that they intended to do before they developed the language in which they succeeded in doing it, was one indication of his break from the tradition of assuming that what was known could always be described clearly, precisely, and exactly. Within his descriptions of his teaching, Joe talked about many instances in which his students were unable to define what they intended to do prior to developing the language that made it possible for them to articulate what they had done. Roberto, for example, was unable to define his intention of creating an *architectural vocabulary* of "tensions between volumes and planes" until he succeeded in creating and testing a *spoken vocabulary* in which he began metaphorically thinking about his "theater spaces" *as* "volumes" and his "hallways and exterior walls" *as* "planes." Roberto's new vocabulary for talking about his theater façade made it possible, for the first time, for him to conceive of his search for a "coherent overall project expression" in terms of the tension between volumes and planes.

For Joe, within the conversations he had with his students, there was no "right" or "wrong" language through which they described their felt intuitions. Their feelings, their spontaneous "animal responses," led to the making of eight quick models, but there was no intention in the making beyond the trust that the models made could (after the fact of their making) be used by their makers as objects to be interpreted, talked about, bandied about, until a spoken set of favorite words, or an unexpected slip of the tongue, resulted in what for the moment sounded like a metaphor that its speaker believed could lead to his personal explanation of why his next design move might be worth pursuing. The intention, as in the poet's process of poem-making, was known only in retrospect. Only as the process of developing one's own language for describing what one wanted to do was retrospectively recognized as the tool that made possible what one had achieved, could one say that he or she *had* an intention. The intention was not there all along. The intention was not discovered. The intention was made as the language for defining the maker's purpose was made.

Playing with Language

If we think of a student designer as one kind of maker, what Joe called the designer's "coherent overall expression" was made within the student designer's search for a "coherent overall expression." Here, Joe's narrative description of his own knowledge within the student-teacher interaction implicated the use of a theory of knowledge in which knowledge was made, rather than discovered. His vocabulary for describing his and his student's knowledge began with the strong poet's premise that knowledge was made individually through a process of developing a language that aligned with one's "own emergent end and purposes."[4] At the same time, Joe recognized that his knowledge about his students' designs, as well as their own knowledge, did not begin with a clear articulation of intentions.

In contrast to the traditional theory of knowledge that supported the idea that if something was known it could be clearly articulated, Joe recognized the student experience of undergoing a state of confusion and inarticulation as a fog that was a natural part of the design process. Rather than negating or diminishing the felt states that his students experienced, Joe supported these initial states by recognizing the transitions from his students' naturally foggy states of nonarticulation into their well-articulated states, by which time the fog had lifted. The fog of inarticulate intuition eventually lifted as his students invented vocabularies (and concurrently made their own knowledge) through a design process in which they tested numerous *in*exact, as opposed to exact, descriptions.

Joe's narrative about his interaction with Roberto was based on the "tension between volumes and planes" language of built forms that Roberto had constructed. Although the word "tension" was an inexact description of his set of eight models, it was a word that throughout his process of testing possible options always pointed him back to his original intuitions about his building design. Joe, throughout his discourse with his students, validated the inexactness of language, especially as language was used to define the students' inner world of vague, and yet unarticulated intuitions, thoughts, and feelings. By speaking about his students' designs within the language that his students had created, Joe made it possible for students to think of him as a teacher who did not control what counted or did not count as a legitimate way to describe their work. Their descriptions, as Joe understood and talked to his students about them, always referred back to the private realm of their feelings, and to their set of life experiences. This implied that there was no right or wrong, but rather, there was description-making within a process of personal emergence.

What Joe controlled in his interaction with his students was the environment in which their vocabulary was most likely to be recognized, by them, as a possibility for defining the big picture, the "parti," the "overall project expression." Roberto's recognition of the possibility of a "balanced tension" rather than an "overpowering tension" between solids and voids in his theater design emerged within the dialogue environment that both he (Roberto) and Joe inhabited. Within that dialogue Joe aimed at using Roberto's set of ideas and metaphors to find out where Roberto was going. Enacting his role as teacher in terms of his students' language was what enabled Joe to freely participate in the formation of his students' designs without them feeling that he was infringing on their status as the "owners and authors" of their designs.

Roberto's acceptance of Joe's interpretation of his (Roberto's) work was not based on Joe's reading of the architectural language that was signified in Roberto's larger "static" model. Rather, Roberto's acceptance was based on Joe's suggestion that the direction, that he (Roberto) had, by then, introduced in the larger model was an abandonment of his earlier direction, in which he had constructed a language of "volumes and planes" to interpret the set of architectural forms within his smaller models. Joe did not judge either direction as better or worse, he simply observed the difference in directions. This allowed Roberto to choose, for himself, which direction he was most interested in pursuing.

Roberto was faced with choosing between the standards that he had originally constructed or the new set of standards that were a departure from his earlier intuitive interest in expressing "the tension between volumes and planes." Joe did not impose his "teacher's standards" for what made a good or bad design. Joe asserted over and over to his students that the language that he was playing with in his conversations with them was *their* language. In turn, students began to acknowledge that they could develop their own set of standards by which to judge in which direction their designs should move next. In the end, Roberto heard and used what Joe told him about the imbalance between the volumes and planes in the larger model because Joe's description fit into the "balanced tension" standard that he (Roberto) had constructed earlier.

Joe's set of teaching practices pointed to the commitment that students could make their own knowledge. Within the process of using their familiar spoken vocabulary to explore the making of a new and unfamiliar vocabulary of architectural forms, his students invented descriptions about their earlier intuitions. Within the process in which students learned to speak an architect's language of forms, Joe emphasized and validated the importance of going back to their vague visceral starting points. By understanding that ideas start as vague, and often indescribable intuitions, Joe legitimized his students' processes of forming incomplete ideas, of cooking up half-baked metaphors, and of stumbling into contradictory explanations. Joe's own way of "figuring out the student's puzzle," a puzzle that he admittedly had to "dig around for" because he "didn't see it right away," reflected the ease with which he played with his students' language and ideas. This validated, for his students, the usefulness of their familiar spoken language within the process of learning a new and unfamiliar architect's language of building forms.

Juggling Descriptions

Embedded within Joe's set of teaching practices was a teaching theory based on the nontraditional idea that knowledge of the world of architecture was made through making descriptions.[5] This nontraditional knowledge theory supported the idea that his students' knowledge of their work changed as their descriptions of their work changed. The old idea that knowledge existed outside of experience in an eternally unchanging state, waiting to be discovered, was abandoned within the vocabulary that Joe used to describe his teaching practices. Knowledge was constantly changing within Joe's interactions with his students, and he validated the "changability of knowledge" by validating the "malleability of the language" that his students (and he) used to describe what was known about the status of his students' building designs. Abandoning the corollary of the traditional knowledge thesis that language had truth imbedded in it, and that language exactly described thought or reality, Joe posed the power of language based on its susceptibility to interpretation and its malleability because of its inexactness.[6] His teaching practices modeled the enactment of the nontraditional knowledge theory through interchanges with his students in which the use of language was based on coming to descriptions that could not at first be known.

Within Joe's narrative of his interactions with his students, he talked about his interest in having his students use their already acquired set of language capacities to make metaphors that referred to their intuitions. These metaphoric reference points could guide them toward the development of an architectural language of building forms that was reflective of the quality of "overall coherence" that their metaphors embodied. For example, one of Joe's students, Farshid, was designing a mixed-use retail and office space building located in a downtown Berkeley block that separated the west and east sides of Shattuck Avenue. In one conversation with Joe, Farshid talked about his intuition that the building design could "weave together the two sides of Shattuck Avenue." The "building as a weave" metaphor that Farshid had invented using his familiar spoken language became the basis for his subsequent invention of a language of architectural forms. Farshid's subsequent architectural language of forms enabled him to design a building that portrayed the kind of "weaving" quality that he had sensed but was unable to articulate in the early phase of his exploration. The architectural expressions of Farshid's "building as weave" manifested through the building's transparency at the sidewalk level (which resulted in a visual connection between the two sides of Shattuck Avenue), through the curvilinear building shape (which resulted in equal accessibility into the building from both street sides), and through his manipulation of building materials in ways that expressed the quality of woven fabric.

Language, within Joe's narrative of his conversations with students, was a tool for inventing personal descriptions of personal experiences. He understood that language *could not* exactly reflect intuitions because personal feelings and intuitions were so vague and indescribable to begin with. But this was a positive aspect of both language and intuition in that it pointed to both being susceptible to many equally valid interpretations. By not posing language as a precision tool that could precisely reflect intuition or thought, Joe validated the role of "making mistakes" within the process of making knowledge. Speaking about their designs in "five different ways," or validating the uniqueness of each of their eight concept models, pointed to Joe's commitment that, as he put it, "sometimes there was no right." When something *was* right, as it was for Roberto, it was based on Roberto's set of self-created standards, not on Joe's externally imposed teacher's standards. Rather than posing the student-teacher interaction with his students in terms where the student was measured against himself as their teacher, Joe posed his relationship with his students based on the terms that they brought into the interaction. Those terms included their set of experiences, language, ideas, and feelings. Joe's method of "knocking at the door until they opened" and his interest in playing with his students' vocabulary by redescribing what they said rather than judging if what they had said was right or wrong, signified an abandonment of the idea that teacher's knowledge (or teacher's vocabulary) was inherently truer, or better, or more useful their students' knowledge.

Joe did not pretend that his descriptions of his students' works were better or truer than his own. Rather, he understood that his experiences, from his vantage point, resulted in his talent for concurrently speaking both the ordinary language (that his students spoke) and his own version of the architect's language of form. By playing with the vocabulary that his students brought into the shared design dialogue that he and they mutually constructed, Joe modeled for his students how to speak about someone else's work (in this case about his student's work) in more ways than just his own. Instead of comparing his students' descriptions of their work in terms of a universal set of timeless architectural standards for what made "good" architecture, Joe engaged in a process of comparing his students' processes with his own process of constructing vocabularies that retrospectively provided descriptions of purpose or knowledge. The comparison of his own descriptions with his students' descriptions came in terms of the process of creating vocabularies, not in terms of which vocabulary was better and which was worse.

Through his teaching, Joe reflected an understanding that his students' capacities to create within the specific domain of architecture came from their already acquired capacity to speak the ordinary language of the world outside of architecture. The validation of his students' self-made knowledge through their self-made vocabularies enabled them to move forward, to navigate through a problem that was entirely new to them. For Joe, personal history, rather than a knowledge of the official history of architecture, was the basis for a student's uniqueness. Joe explained that his belief that his students' past experiences were all they needed to drive their studio explorations paralleled his belief that a knowledge of architectural history was not a necessary prerequisite to learning design. He told me, "I think by the time we are twenty, twenty-one years old, that we have enough sense of architecture and planning and formal qualities of space that we can design without actually studying history. Now there may be parallels to other people's work that they may want to investigate but I don't think it is necessary to do that first: to stuff your head with magazines and come in and try to design. In fact I think it is wrong. For me, personally, anyways. But I do believe that each person has within them unique experiences that will lead to something interesting for us all to learn from in their work."

Believing that each of his students had a unique set of experiences that drove their personal set of interests and intuitions about design, problems, Joe had created a set of teaching approaches in which he actively engaged in listening for his students' voices. At the same time that Joe practiced what Coyne and Snodgrass described as "being actively involved in the development of the design ideas of others."[7] Joe did not take himself out of the picture that he constructed as he described his interactions with his students. He defined the teacher-student learning interaction as "co-designing," a process in which his role as a designer was not posed in terms of his authoritative status at a level that diminished his students' knowledge. Rather, he saw his role as a *dialogue partner* who brought into the teaching act an interest in both his own and his students' design vocabularies within an interactive conversation.

As opposed to the old idea that the kind of knowledge that the student possessed was distinct from the kind that teachers had, Joe validated the equivalent status of both participants' knowledge-making processes by speaking about his students' works based on the development of their design ideas. Joe practiced what Eudora Welty described as *listening for,* as opposed to *listening to,* a story.[8] Within the learning relationship with his students, Joe listened for the person they embodied by listening for his students' stories and for the vocabularies they chose to speak within their attempt at making their felt inner lives known.[9] Joe listened for the inward significance of his students' situations: for the vocabulary, the set of words, phrases, and metaphors that signified their alternative conception (as compared to his own conception) of their designs.

In the end Joe recognized *both* his own and his students' vocabularies as legitimate descriptions of the same objective design reality. He did *not* resist the idea that there could be many ways to describe his students' works, or that there could be many truths that could explain one design. He understood that there was no one standard for a student's intellectual or bodily ways of making knowledge of the world for themselves. His use of his own vocabulary of architectural form-making was not posed to students in terms of a better or higher or more powerful vocabulary, but rather he posed his architect's language as one of many types of vocabularies (including the student's own) that could be used within the search for a design project's coherency. In the new pedagogical game that Joe played, he and his students shared and compared descriptions. Within their new game, talent, rather than being defined as the ability to clearly articulate why the architecture one had created was "good" or "bad," was defined as the ability to juggle, to keep in the air, as many different languages as there were creators participating in the act of designing.

Chapter Six

Gina: The Complexity of Difference

Letting Go of Convention

One of things I noticed during my elevator rides up to architect Gina Vismara's sixth floor beginning design studio was a distinct difference between the kinds of things that students carried with them during the official 1 to 6 p.m. studio hours *and* the kinds of things that they tended to carry with them during their late night, or overnight, studio stays. During my afternoon rides up to Gina's studio I noticed students carrying models, drawings, assorted architectural tools-of-the-trade, as well as their backpacks, notebooks, sketchbooks, Walkmans, and compact disc players. In contrast, the after-hours elevator riders carried a variety of food stuffs that would be used to sustain them through the "all nighter" stints common within the culture of architecture studios during the night before a project deadline. These late nighters carried their dinners of rice and sweet and sour pork, or steak and melted cheese sandwiches, or pepperoni pizza, bottles of Evian drinking water, cans of Coke and Pepsi, bars of chocolate, packages of M and M's, boxes of Triscuits, and most often cups of coffee or espresso or mocha or latte from the Cafe Strada.

Compared to the generous portions of dinner, and the large quantities of sugared products and caffeinated beverages that students needed to "pull all-nighters," the brown bag lunches that Gina and I brought to our series of recorded conversations were modest and light. A chicken salad sandwich, a take-out order of sushi, a bottle of Kiwi-Strawberry Snapple, a bag of "Sun Chips," or a banana, or an apple were typical items on our lunchtime menus. Gina's schedule was very tight, and as it turned out, lunchtime was the best time for her to squeeze-in our series of conversations about her way of teaching.

In a small, quiet meeting room on the third floor of Wurster Hall, where we met for lunch and conversation, Gina often emphasized her interest in teaching her twelve students "how to be independent in their designs." Expanding on what she meant by "independence" in the work of architectural design students, Gina told me that as opposed to a "non-humanities" perspective on teaching, in which students were expected to come up with "pretty much the same" answer to problems, she expected that each of her students would produce work that was "completely different" from their peers. She described her pedagogical interests in terms of teaching toward "difference" and "individual type of work as opposed to sameness."

"I get very worried when I see sameness in the studio," Gina told me as she described her students' struggles with "letting go of conventions, of norms, and of what is expected." She understood her students' resistance to "letting go" as the roadblock that kept them from "incorporating" their "individual talents, differences, and strengths" into their work. For Gina the process of "letting go of convention" (of getting away from sameness) was concurrent with her students' processes of recognizing their own individuality and difference. One of the primary conventions that Gina believed that students could eventually "let go of" was the traditional language that architects spoke. But before "letting go of" conventional language, before, as she put it, "venturing into uncharted territory," students had to "not only know themselves as individuals, but also become secure about their knowledge about the convention of architectural language."

For Gina, the students' process of developing their own individual sense of who they were as designers started with acknowledging the conventions, the traditional vocabulary and metaphors, that were part of the language spoken by the architects who inhabited the design world of Wurster Hall. Once they understood the normal and conventional ways that architects had adopted for talking about the design and construction of buildings, then students could "start inventing new ways of communicating" through a process of "manipulating" the existing conventional language. The "letting go" of convention interlocked with the students' recognition of their individuality and difference, and these two aspects of the design process, in turn, interlocked with their process of "manipulating conventional architectural language."

Within Gina's narrative of studio teaching and learning, the manipulation of language, the creation of building designs, and the recognition of individuality and self were coincident and interlocking processes. She told me she believed that "the best work came from the sort of personal or inner self," and that she, as a teacher, could recognize her students' "personal, inner selves" in their work when they "started believing in their work, and started defending it on its own grounds." "I think it happens in small ways," she told me, referring to her students' process of learning to believe in, and defending, their work, "but even at this early level where I may tell a student 'Maybe you should look at it this way or that way,' and they will say 'No, that wouldn't be consistent with my idea.' That's when I go, 'oh great.' The personality of the designer is starting to be formed and I nurture that."

Personal Meanings and Memories

The formative stages of developing an individual personality as a designer interlocked with a process in which students learned the conventions of architectural language so that they could "manipulate" that language in their own individual and different ways. Gina related her students' processes of learning to recognize and make use of their own individuality and difference to her own experience of leaving her native Italian culture to come to the United States, or more specifically, to come to Berkeley for her undergraduate architectural studies. She conveyed her experience of simultaneously entering into the foreign cultures of the United States and the architectural culture of Wurster Hall, telling me, "I came from a place where everybody knew me, to this place where I was nobody. I mean that could be incredibly intimidating because it's in Berkeley, California, in the United States. Not only was I foreign to the culture, but I was also foreign to this place, to this school. So in order to kind of swim or sink, I really concentrated on fulfilling the requirements just like my students do. To be a really good student. That's what I knew how to do no matter what the cultural milieu, so I did that because I didn't know anything else. And I survived."

For Gina, surviving the intimidation of finding herself in the "foreign culture" of architecture school was a matter of "being a good student" because she "didn't know how to do anything else," and was not a matter of finding the "sort of personal or inner self" that she defined as the basis that enabled architects to create their "best work." She related her past experiences as a beginning design student to the current experiences with her own students, telling me, "I think in my undergraduate education I was too concerned (and I think most of those kids are concerned) about convincing myself that I could be an architect proving to me and to others that I did have what it took." But the "proof" that she "had what it took" to be an architect came through surviving the system and adopting the conventions of traditional architectural language rather than coming to "an awareness" of who she was as an architect; an awareness she believed enabled the confidence required to "let go" of existing architectural language conventions.

That awareness came for Gina during the time that she was an architecture graduate student at Yale University. It was there that she realized "that the best work came out of a personal search," as opposed to producing work that although it might have been "well crafted and well represented, had no soul." For Gina, design work that "had soul" was reflective of a designer's "personal search." That search was informed by a designer's "interests" and a sense of "who she was." At Yale, Gina found for the first time that by incorporating "political issues, issues of gender, and issues of race" into her design works she could define who she was both as an architect *and* as a person. Put another way, she found that she could express her personal voice through her design creations. Although her "awareness of her personal self" came during her graduate experience , Gina told me "I don't see why that awareness couldn't come in undergraduate school, and that's what I try to teach my students."

Of the several design projects that her students completed during the summer session in which I observed Gina, the "room project" was the one that she felt best conveyed her pedagogical approach to challenging her students to "let go" of architectural language conventions by creating designs reflective of their inner selves. In the "room project" students had to choose three objects that would be the starting points for their investigations into the design of a room that was meant to function in much the same way that their existing bedrooms functioned: as spaces in which they kept their possessions, where they slept, and where they did their studying. The aim of having students choose three objects to be housed in the room was to have them recognize that objects evoked personal meanings and memories that could inform the direction of their designs.

Within her conversations with her students, Gina responded to descriptions in which they revealed how the personal meanings that their selected objects had evoked for them were informing the architectural language of forms that they were developing as they moved forward in their designs. "I love the room project," Gina said enthusiastically, "because it is so transparent. They can't get away from self. It's a very good way to get at the core of the student and some of their preoccupations. This is something that they know about and they can talk about."

Ernesto: "People Wouldn't Understand"

One example of the use that Gina made of her students' "preoccupations" was conveyed as she told me about a desk crit conversation she had had with Ernesto, a twenty-year-old Latino man in her design studio. Gina reflected on her conversation with Ernesto, telling me, "He initially wanted to include reproductions of Diego Rivera murals in his room, and he decided against it, and I said, 'Why?' And he said, 'because people wouldn't understand.' So I said, 'Because it's the work of Diego Rivera's murals? Do you mean that you were thinking that an Anglo-Saxon person could not understand, could not get at the core of the work? There is an exhibit going on right now at the Museum of Modern Art on that very subject, Diego Rivera and Frida Kahlo, and maybe you should go. It is the height of high culture and there it is. And next door across the street there is a Center for the Arts that was created for the very purpose to showcase multicultural art in the city, in the Bay Area: to really look at some of our own artists and what they are talking about.' So that was one glimpse that I got."

Gina had gotten "a glimpse" of "the core" of Ernesto's individual identity as a designer via his description of his personal interest in Diego Rivera's artwork. She took Ernesto's intimation about his hesitancy to make use of the Rivera poster as a cue that he needed validation of the anxiety he felt about being a Latino in an "Anglo-Saxon" culture. Her affirmation of Rivera as a Latino artist whose works had been culturally approved as being "the height of high culture," and her subsequent affirmation of local "multicultural art" was her way of posing that she perceived Ernesto's cultural difference as a strength to be pursued through *ex*pression, rather than diminished or discounted through *re*pression.

While Ernesto eventually abandoned the use of the poster of the Diego Rivera mural as one of his "room project" objects, he began developing an architectural vocabulary in which he employed colored wall surfaces that Gina described as similar to those of Mexican architect Luis Barragan. Ernesto may have been implicitly revealing his Latino identity through the use of "Barragan" kinds of color schemes, but he was among the majority of students who, in Gina's experience as an undergraduate design teacher, had not acquired the confidence to "go out on a limb" and explicitly explore the relationship between their cultural identities or their inner selves *and* their design vocabularies. She explained, "Only very rarely have I had undergraduate students that have done that. And I am very encouraging of that, always. If they want to bring cultural themes to their work, hey, as long as they work within the parameters of the studio that's just the more richer. So I am often very encouraging of that but not everybody has that self-confidence to take that leap and do something different than the others."

Gina's "nurturance" of Ernesto's difference, his uniqueness, was meant to point him in the direction of "doing something different than the others," of defining his own set of architectural metaphors that reflected his inner self and his "awareness" of the architect that he was becoming. But despite Gina's encouragement, Ernesto chose to abandon the use of the Rivera poster as the starting point in his design exploration; a use that would have explicitly revealed what she called the "cognizance of his identity." Instead he opted to safely imitate a previously created architectural vocabulary of color and form. The possibility of explicitly expressing his cultural identity had been eclipsed by his lack of confidence and his fear of being misunderstood. Imitating the style of Barragan, an architect whose Latino cultural roots were aligned with Ernesto's own, may have seemed to Ernesto to have been a step in the direction of expressing his unique identity, but in the end, he had created a replica rather than a set of architectural metaphors that were particularly his own. Gina's encouragement and validation of Ernesto's own expressions of cultural and personal self were aimed at shoring up the confidence that he would need if he was to eventually break from the conventional design language that he, instead, chose to replicate.

Julia: Translating Metaphor Into Space

Another student she spoke about within her narratives of her teaching experiences in her beginning design studio pointed to Gina's pedagogical aim of encouraging her students to "go out on a limb" by making use of their own interests and their own metaphors within their individual design processes. Gina described Julia, an Asian American woman in her early twenties, as a student who "had an incredible ability to translate metaphor kinds of concepts into spaces." Julia revealed her "incredible ability" by thinking of one of her "room project" objects as a metaphor for the kinds of experienced qualities she wanted her room to exhibit. Thinking and speaking metaphorically about the candle she had chosen as one of her "room project" objects helped guide Julia toward the development of her own architectural language of building forms and spaces.

Gina explained Julia's process of using a candle to guide a meta-phorical exploration of architectural space, recalling that "there was a moment early on when Julia was talking about the flicker of a candle and how that translated into space." Julia had produced a sketch in which she attempted to render an interior quality reminiscent of the experience of candlelight. As she talked about her sketch of the room Julia described her interest in designing a room in which various intensities of light, from bright light to dark shadow, could be experienced as the inhabitants of the room moved from the room's periphery to its interior.

As she spoke to Gina, Julia likened the architectural qualities of light intensity dissipating from bright to dim *and* the contrasting light and dark shadow play on wall surfaces *to* the experiential qualities of a flickering candle. At that point in her design process, Julia had stopped thinking and talking about the candle as an object and started thinking and talking about the candle as a metaphor. The arrangement of walls, the size and location of windows, and the types of building materials needed were talked about in terms of the support they could lend to the experiential quality that the "flickering candle" metaphor suggested.

Julia had entered into a first stage of developing an original vocabulary for talking about the actual forms and building materials that would support the "flickering candle" effect that she was exploring. She told Gina about her interest in positioning a series of interior walls parallel with one of the room's exterior walls. Light that came into the room from a large exterior window would then penetrate through "small openings in the interior walls." Through this configuration the space adjacent to a large exterior window would be brightest, and the succeeding spaces (separated by interior walls punctured by small openings) would be less and less bright *but* more and more "flickering."

Gina recalled coming into the studio two days after she and Julia had explored ways in which Julia's set of architectural forms (walls, windows, and adjacent spaces) could be used to create a space that evoked the feeling of "a flickering candle." But by that time Julia had abandoned the "flickering candle" as the metaphorical basis for her design and was exploring what Gina described as "trellis type things with the columns marking the rhythm" of the experienced progres-sion from the exterior wall to the interior center of the room. In other words, Julia had abandoned the idea of using a candle-like dissipation of light to mark the progression from a space adjacent to the exterior of the room *to* a space at the center of the room. Instead, as Gina put it, she (Julia) had opted for "something more conventional." Julia had dropped her development of an original vocabulary of architectural ways to describe progression through *light,* and instead began employing a conventional way of marking progression through space by using the traditional architectural vocabulary of *columns.*

Gina told me that when she asked Julia why she had abandoned her original "flickering candle" metaphor and concurrent exploration of architectural forms, Julia told her that "she didn't think that it had a practical use. She didn't think that one could inhabit that kind of space. Julia asked me 'What kind of program, what kind of use could happen here?' This is why she just "X"ed it. And I felt like saying, 'Who cares about the use? You know, it's beautiful.' And I said, 'Julia it doesn't have to be the entire room. It could have been a moment in the passage, it could have been a way of designing the space.' You see I feel that just as much as you can derive form from program you can also do it the other way around. You can have a form and think about a program: a way to use it. She had never been in a space like that. It didn't recall any other space she had been to before. So she said, 'forget it, this is no good.' I think she has got great sensibility. To me that says that she's got talent and that she should develop it, that she should push it."

When I asked Gina why she thought Julia had not "pushed it," but rather, had abandoned her original "flickering candle" metaphor, she said, "Maybe it's peer pressure. Other people who look at her desk and they are not understanding. Conventions, norms, what is expected. I don't know who the kind of judging is for her. Is it what is published in the magazines? Her peers? Her past teachers?" Recalling the "moment early on" when Julia seemed to be on her way to making use of her "sensibility" for "translating metaphor kinds of concepts into spaces," Gina framed Julia's subsequent abandonment as "the syndrome of having a lucid moment and being able to create something wonderful and then "X"ing it out because it's not practical."

Worries About Sameness

The "lucid moment" that Julia had experienced was understood by Gina as a moment that signified the beginnings of a process in which the young designer had started inventing her own set of metaphors for talking about, and making, her design. What Gina had seen in Julia's initial "flickering candle" description was the possibility that Julia's "lucid moment," which led her to the invention of a metaphoric vocabulary, could sustain her throughout the process of developing an architectural vocabulary that was just as "lucid." Gina had supported Julia's initial metaphoric exploration of her room design, but although Julia had invented spoken terms for talking about her design ideas, she had never experienced the kind of space that she was attempting to design, and therefore she was unable to exactly describe, in architectural terms, what she wanted to do.

The problem, as Gina saw it, was that the metaphor that Julia had invented for initiating her design exploration was not of the conventional type that easily aligned with any conventional architectural vocabulary of building forms or materials. Gina recalled what she had told Julia about the process of starting out with a "lucid" but unconventional vocabulary and then attempting to translate that vocabulary into architectural terms: "I told her that she should be less concerned with the conventional. That she still has a very hard time abandoning convention. I mean she wants to, but she won't. So I said, 'Just take the risk. I mean you have the sensibility. Even if you are not entirely sure where you are going, explore it. And give it a chance." Because that idea was only two days old and then she "X"ed it."

By defending design ideas in *her own* metaphoric terms, Julia had sent Gina a clear signal that her (Julia's) "designer personality" was being formed. Julia had taken the risk of constructing her own design vocabulary. She had manipulated a candle as an object through the poetic process of likening qualities of objects to qualities of other objects. In this case likening the luminescent qualities of a candle to the spatial qualities of a room. Julia's "sensibilities" for manipulating spoken language were, at the same time, signs of her potential talent for manipulating the architectural language of building forms and materials. Gina's telling Julia, "you have the sensibility," was her teacher's way of validating that her students already possessed one of the essential requisites for manipulating architectural language: the talent for manipulating ordinary spoken language. She treated the language capabilities that her students brought with them to her studio as reflections of their inner selves. By framing the processes of manipulating ordinary spoken language as "simultaneous with" the processes of manipulating form and space, Gina conveyed to her students the possibility that creating architecture was coincident with the architect's discovery of her self.

From Gina's pedagogical viewpoint, Julia's "incredible ability to translate metaphor kinds of concepts into spaces" could lead to Julia's best design work if, and when, Julia realized that through the design process she could define who she was both as an architect *and* as a person. Gina realized that Julia's strength as a metaphor maker could be used to overcome what Harold Bloom recognized as the strong poet's "anxiety of influence": the poet's fear of replicating other poets' conventions, and thus never creating a work that was uniquely one's own.[1] Gina's encouraging Julia to be "less concerned with the conventional," and to "take risks even when not entirely sure where she was going," was indicative of a teacher who believed that her students could overcome their tendency toward conventional ways of creating buildings and conventional ways of exhibiting designer personalities that were imitations of others rather than expressions of their own unique voices and vocabularies.

Gina's "worry about sameness in the studio" ultimately referred to the creative makers' recognition that their processes of creating were synchronous with their processes of discovering their selves. Gina's support of her students' attempts at "letting go of convention" reflected her belief that her students could invent interlocking linguistic and architectural vocabularies that were their own. Students like Ernesto and Julia were not problematic for Gina because, although they ultimately abandoned their initial design ideas and vocabularies in favor of more conventional approaches, they nonetheless revealed what Gina called "moments of conviction in the work." For Gina even a fleeting "moment of conviction" (a moment when a student argued for a design based on his or her own ideas) was a sign that a student could, over time, develop a set of design process habits that reflected his or her ability to "work independently," "let go of convention," and discover his or her "inner self."

Catherine: Vocabularies Not Her Own

Of all her students, Gina found Catherine the most frustrating because, as Gina described it, there was "not a moment of conviction in her work." As opposed to the minimal "worry about sameness" that Gina felt about Ernesto's and Julia's immature fear of the unconventional, the "sameness" that frustrated Gina about Catherine manifested in the form of Catherine's tendency to "regurgitate the same idea over and over." Gina believed that Catherine's tendency toward constant repetition of the same design idea was rooted in her "thinking that she was completely unable to come up with something new." As a result of her perceived inability to have original design ideas, Gina told me that Catherine was "much more prone to say, 'I saw that example in *Architectural Digest*. I think I'm going to employ it right here' as opposed to saying 'what is enclosure?' or 'How do we define passage?' "

Gina expanded on her frustration with Catherine. As she started with a deep sigh she explained, "The only one I'm really worried about is Catherine. She is very stubborn. She has these preconceived ideas. Somewhere along the line she has been used to, she has gotten used to praise. Somebody must have been doing a lot of patting on her back, and saying, 'Oh it's beautiful, oh wow, just go that way.' There is no way I'm going to tell her that and since I'm not going to give her that, then she's gone through twenty variations of her scheme. She is just waiting for this standing ovation and she cannot get that conviction from herself. She cannot work independently. It's unbelievable. Not a moment of conviction in the work. It's almost like," Gina changed from her adult tone to imitate a child's voice, and ended her characterization with, "did you like this, can I do this?"

Gina equated Catherine's lack of independence to her absolute inability to generate her own design ideas. To compensate for her impotence in original design thinking Catherine reverted to cutting and pasting the works of others into her own work. The problem with Catherine's mode of aping the ideas of other designers, as Gina described it, originated "somewhere along the line" when she had been uncritically praised for her efforts. The result of Catherine having sought and apparently having received her previous teachers' approvals was that Catherine had developed the habit of believing that if she kept generating "variations on her scheme" she would eventually hit upon a design that would move her teachers to applaud her efforts with a "standing ovation."

Given Gina's pedagogical approach through which students learned to draw upon their inner personal selves as the basis that enabled them to move beyond convention toward their own original design vocabularies, Catherine's stubborn reliance on design vocabularies that were ostensibly not her own was problematic. It was within the "room project" that Gina gained insight into Catherine's habitual tendency toward the conventional. One of the objects that Catherine had chosen to house within her "room project" design was (as she explained to Gina) the diploma that she would eventually receive upon completion of her undergraduate studies. Through her desk crit conversations with Catherine, Gina began to "put her finger on" the personal meaning that the diploma had evoked for Catherine.

Gina told me, "It's very interesting that one of her objects was the diploma. And it was such a big deal about the diploma. Catherine is highly conventional in the sense that she is doing it for the degree, not for the education. She is not in the thinking, in exploring, and spending sleepless nights thinking about exactly how do you feel when you walk through this building. She's interested in, 'By the time 1998 is over,' she says, 'I graduated Berkeley.' I think I'm finally starting to put my finger on it. I think it's about consuming. I think that is what I find so troubling: it's about acquiring.

"The degree is one more of her possessions in a certain sense. And I hate to, I know I'm standing on pretty shaky ground making a value judgment on her social status or her background, but I know enough about her as a person that I cannot help but make conclusions and put two and two together. I think the degree is just one more acquisition. That's what really irks me, because that's the particular kind of person that I am. Education, for me, is a sort of a whole category apart. And it has to do with a lot of my background. For me it's in a category all its own. In other words, it doesn't matter to me how much you make, if you are not well educated then it's not important... Education is a way to skip social classes. The fact that you were born into a certain social class shouldn't mark you for life. That if you have ambition, and you are tenacious enough that's a bridge. And it is perhaps the only kind of democratic space, the space of education. So for somebody to be treating the degree as a commodity is very insulting."

From Gina's particular point-of-view, the "glimpse" that she had caught of Catherine's "core" brought into focus a picture of a student whose "social status" habits of acquiring and consuming led her to treat her undergraduate degree "as a commodity." For Catherine, her undergraduate degree would be "one more of her possessions." As opposed to viewing a higher education diploma as a "commodity," Gina saw it as part of the democratic promise that those with ambition and tenacity could eventually "bridge" beyond the class that they were born into. Catherine's "highly conventional" attitude toward her education, her "doing it for the degree, not for the education," irked and insulted Gina, but at the same time it helped explain why Catherine was "not in the thinking" or the "exploring" modes of designing that were characteristic of other students in Gina's studio.

In contrast to her other students, who showed some degree of commitment to their own ideas by defending their designs based on personal terms that they had invented to guide their explorations, for Catherine there were "no moments of conviction." Gina's frustrations with, and worries about, Catherine emerged in response to what Gina described as Catherine's stubborn adherence to a method of rearranging the pieces of other designers' works, her habit of relying on her previous teachers' approvals of designs that were devoid of original ideas, and the absence of conviction to her own ideas as the driving force behind her work. Gina's worries and frustrations about Catherine's lack of originality, and her ways of compensating for that lack, were signs of Gina's commitment that her students could become designers whose work was composed of their own original vocabularies, which expressed who they were as persons and who they could be as professionals.

Moments of Conviction

Within her narrative of herself and her students, Gina posed herself as a teacher who validated her students' unique experiences; she validated their personal interests and cultural roots as the source of the knowledge that existed within them. By validating her students' cultural backgrounds, unique experiences, and individual talents as the bases for their designs, Gina shifted the conversations with them away from the traditional focus on the teacher as the official in charge of policing what counted or did not count as true knowledge of architecture.

As opposed to putting herself in the position of playing the teacher who pretended to know what good architecture was or was not, Gina challenged her students to create designs that were reflective of knowledge that existed within their inner selves. Instead of judging their work based on a set of universal standards for what made certain architecture good and other architecture bad, Gina challenged her students to define for themselves their own metaphoric standards. By initiating their design explorations based on metaphors that they had authored, only the students could judge whether or not their interlocking set of linguistic and architectural vocabularies were reflective of the discoveries they had made about themselves in the process of creating and testing those vocabularies. For Gina her students' "moments of conviction" signaled their awareness of the connection between the person they were deep inside and the designs that they were creating. Moments when students displayed a confidence comprised of both their commitment to the vocabulary they had created to guide their explorations *and* their commitment to the unique set of interests that sustained that vocabulary's originality were moments when their "designer personality" was being discovered.

One of Gina's recurring messages to her students was that defining and making explicit their differences, their individuality, was an essential first step toward creating their own set of original metaphors: metaphors that would define who they uniquely were both as architects and persons. Gina exemplified a teacher attempting to break from the traditional premise that the students' adequacy was measured by comparing what they knew to what their teacher knew. By insisting that individual difference was the source of individual knowledge, and individual knowledge was the basis for design explorations, Gina attempted to diffuse the tradition of comparing her students to herself.

Metaphoric Dissonance

In Gina's design studio, the students' use of individual differences was based on them recognizing their uniqueness by creating metaphors that were as particular and unique as they were. But Gina's approach to having her students recognize and use their unique perspectives to inform their processes of inventing original design metaphors broke down when her students' personal metaphors affronted the "particular kind of person that she was." Here I refer to Gina's narrative of her interactions with Catherine. Within Gina's narrative, Catherine's personal metaphoric equation, in which a *diploma* equated to *status*, contradicted her (Gina's) metaphor in which *a diploma* equated to *democratic equity*. By invalidating Catherine's metaphoric construction of diploma as status symbol, as compared to her different metaphoric construction of diploma as democratic symbol, Gina had enacted just the kind of traditional pedagogical practice that she seemed to genuinely want to break free of. She had overlooked the possibility that Catherine's metaphor could have become the basis of her (Catherine's) design exploration, in much the same way that Julia's "flickering candle" metaphor sustained her initial design investigation.

Gina's oversight was informative because it pointed to a set of complications that often emerged for teachers who, like Gina, were committed to breaking free of the inherited notion that a student's individual differences, her unique identity and her past experiences, were deterrents within a process in which she was expected to learn to speak her teacher's language. Breaking free of the tradition that the student's adequacy could be measured only in terms of how much the student knew in comparison to what the teacher already knew began with the commitment that what was known was what the knowers had discovered about themselves. The role that difference played within this new theory, that knowledge was self-knowledge, was based on the uses that could be made by comparing differences without looking for something inherent that made one more or less adequate than the others. Rather than thinking that a difference of opinion, or a different way of life, or a different metaphoric use of diploma, could be resolved by determining whose difference made them better or worse, difference marked the start of a dialogue in which participants actively listened for contrast, contradiction, misinterpretation, or (as was the case with Catherine and Gina) metaphoric dissonance.[2]

By emphasizing the role that the inner lives of students had within their design explorations, Gina showed her interest in abandoning the idea that knowledge was something to be discovered outside of personal experience. But she went only half-way toward making a clean break from traditional ways of theorizing *both* knowledge *and* the teacher-student learning relationship because instead of dropping the idea that knowledge was discovered, she replaced the idea of discovering knowledge *outside of* the self with the idea of discovering knowledge *inside of* the self. The half she completed was in thinking that knowledge did not exist outside of her students' inner selves, and this commitment was conveyed through her interest in nurturing and supporting her students' recognition of their difference by discovering who they were on the inside and how their inner selves could drive their design explorations.

What Gina overlooked was that in thinking that knowledge was discovered (regardless of whether it was discovered on the inside or the outside of the self) she was implicitly committing to the traditional idea that certain methods of discovering knowledge, or certain vocabularies for talking about what had been discovered, were more or less adequate than others. As a result of going only half way toward the abandonment of the traditional knowledge discovered thesis, Gina overlooked the possibility that differences between her and her students' metaphors, when recognized as a positive force, could have been used to drive her interactions with her students. The discrepancies between her and her students' differing metaphors might have been used as starting points toward exploring design issues in which architectural form related to status, or building fenestration related to democratic iconography, or the built symbols of status were related to built symbols of democracy.

The metaphoric dissonance could have called both Gina's and Catherine's attention to the opportunity for each to share experiences that underlay their contrasting views. At one point in our conversations, Gina told me about a time she had called Catherine to inform her of a final review schedule and had gotten a phone machine message in which Catherine (whose family owned a diving instruction school in Santa Cruz, California) talked about upcoming diving classes. "The terminology" that Catherine used to describe various diving categories on the phone message was, as Gina put it, "very foreign" sounding to her ears. Perhaps the vocabulary of "diving terminology" was just as foreign sounding to Gina's ears as the vocabulary of architectural form and design was to Catherine's ears. Gina's own experienced "intimidation" during her immersion into a foreign American culture might have been one of many starting points in the conversation in which metaphoric dissonance could have been viewed as a vehicle for mutually constructing the dialogue between Catherine and herself.

Gina's consistent interest in having her students develop what she described as the "self-confidence to take that leap and do something different than the others," pointed to her validating and nurturing her students' inventions of their own original vocabularies for talking about, and making, their designs. Her set of teaching practices pointed her students to the underlying premise that their processes of designing were synchronous with their processes of learning to make descriptions of themselves in their own terms. While Gina's narrative of her interactions with her students implicated a nontraditional educational theory in which personal knowledge (as opposed to objective impersonal knowledge) was a valid source of design making *and* metaphor making, her narrative also revealed the complexities of difference that emerged when she experienced a *metaphoric dissonance* within particular interactions with particular students.

Gina's annoyance with students whose metaphors suggested to her that their vocabularies were less valid as compared to her own could be taken as a sign of her inconsistent commitment to the development of a set of teaching practices that were based on honoring individual difference. *But,* it could *also* be taken to mean that inconsistencies are bound to emerge within the process of testing out new educational vocabularies and practices. This challenges teachers to understand that facing and acknowledging personal inconsistencies is part of the process of breaking free of the habits that have consciously or unconsciously supported their previously held set of conventional practices and traditional educational vocabularies. Gina pointed to the first step in that process: the courage to venture into uncharted educational practice territory where previously untried methods could be tested. The complexities, inconsistencies, ambiguities, and contradictions that pointed back to the very educational conventions that Gina sought to abandon could be understood as part of a process in which revisiting one's traditional place of educational pedagogy, acknowledging the old set of habits that one has developed as a long-time resident of that place, and understanding the origins of old vocabularies that one learned to speak while inhabiting that place are the first steps that, in the long run, might eventually lead to leaving that place behind.

Chapter Seven

For the Beginnings

Thinking Education Metaphorically

Designing and building buildings is a process that brings together the speakers of many different vocabularies. The carpenter, the plumber, the glazier, the electrician, the roofer, and the mason each speak a different sort of language about the planning and construction of buildings. Historically, architects were thought of as the uniquely qualified translators of the multiple vocabularies within the design and construction process, translators who were able to bring order to a conference whose participants spoke in such different tongues. Their ability to converse freely with speakers of numerous vocabularies was seen as one of the architect's chief assets. Architects were valued because they understood each specialist's unique language. Following the architect's own tradition of conversing freely with speakers of numerous vocabularies, my series of conversations with three architects who taught beginning design studios were undertaken as part of an investigation that could lead to a perspective of education as seen from the teacher's point-of-view, and as heard from each teacher's unique pedagogical vocabulary.

My qualitative analysis of three design educators' vocabularies, which comprise this chapter, was also undertaken in the spirit of an architectural form of thinking, a form of thinking that was recognized and associated with architectural thinking as far back as the Roman era. More than two millennia ago, Vitruvius noted with interest, the architect's ability to think about things in terms of other things. Buildings succeed, he suggested, when the architect resisted focusing on any one special aspect of the building and instead kept in mind all of the building's multiple aspects. The critical aspects of building design that the successful architect had to compare, contrast, and concurrently consider, according to Vitruvius, were *venustas, utilitas,* and *firmitas,* which we moderns translated as beauty, function, and structure.[1] Today, we define the architect's mode of thinking about certain aspects of the building relative to other aspects as *metaphorical thinking*.

Metaphorical thinking and speaking (thinking or speaking of one thing in terms of another) drives the architect's mode of practice today in much the same way that it fueled the Roman architects' designs in their antique era. For example, when architects today speak about *form* in terms of *function*, they are using their metaphoric mode *of connecting by contrasting* in a way that reflects their Roman ancestors' use of metaphor when they spoke about *venustas* in terms of *utilitas*. The architect's capacity for talking about form in terms of function, or structure in terms of economy, or economy in terms of beauty, or their capacity for metaphorical thought, often come into play within the design process. Within the process of designing and building buildings, problems emerge that call for thinking of windows in terms of doors, or of lighting in terms of plumbing. It also calls for relating the mason's job to the carpenter's, or the carpenter's job to the electrician's. The different building parts and the different people who play a part in the building process may appear to be unrelated, *but* they are just the things and people that architects spend their time relating. Thinking of one aspect of the building in terms of another helps architects determine how numerous building parts need to join up with one another. Thinking of the specialist's vocabulary in terms of their own vocabulary helps architects to integrate new ideas, products, and technologies that come from outside of the architectural domain into the domain of building design and construction. It is the architect's metaphorical mode of thinking that points in the direction of those places where different building parts intersect and where different vocabularies converge.

In the preceding chapters I introduced you to the vocabularies that each of three teachers relied upon to frame their respective descriptions of their learning relationships with students in their beginning design studios. In this chapter, following the metaphorical mode that architects have historically employed, I analyzed each of these teacher's individual vocabularies relative to the other two. This analysis, then, was a *metaphorical* study of teachers' vocabularies in the sense that one teacher's teaching practice vocabulary was analyzed in terms of the others. I found that the metaphors of educational practice that emerged within each of these three teachers' narrative vocabularies were a useful shorthand way to capture each of their approaches within the beginning design studio. The juxtaposition of the various metaphors that each teacher used in framing a particular set of pedagogical practices led to a set of starting points that could guide future conversations on educative processes. That set of points will be presented following the analysis of the theory-implicit narratives of the three teachers who participated in this investigation.

Separation and Control

The three teachers' reflections on their design studio pedagogies were compared and contrasted in terms of the theory of knowledge embedded within their narratives, in terms of their descriptions of their image of themselves as teachers, and in terms of their explanation of their students' learning processes. For example, recall that Manny Bradley told me that "much of the teaching I attempt to do starts with the proposition that we are going to construct a dialogue that is as objective as we can make it. That we are going to work very hard to get outside of "I want, I like." Manny's metaphor for his interaction with students was the "construction of an objective dialogue." His "objective dialogue" metaphor for his teaching was invented to help explain his practice of disallowing the students within his design studio to speak in the first person "I." The exclusion of student usage of such phrases as "I want" or "I like" was posed as part of his set of interlocking theses about knowledge that began with the premise that knowledge that was useful within designing was knowledge that emerged from the student's "capacity to think, and to reason, and to argue and persuade."

Students who used the first person "I" signaled that they had not yet reached, or did not have the capacity to reach, an objective reasoning "level of thought." Manny's thesis that the only legitimate kind of knowledge was the unbiased "reasoning" type interlocked with his thesis that knowledge came in levels: a higher objective level and the lower level of opinion. The thesis that knowledge came in levels, in turn, interlocked with the educational thesis that students who could reason dispassionately were at a higher level of knowledge, as compared to students who, because they relied on their reactive, unreflective, "self-indulgent" opinions, were at a lower level of knowledge. Within his "construction of an objective dialogue" metaphor for beginning design studio education, Manny posed his teacher's role in terms of his attempt at weaning his students off of their previous self-indulgent habits of relying on their personal interests and values to inform their designs. He emphasized his teacher's interest in inducing his students into "making the reversal" *from* developing design vocabularies based on personal wants and likes *to* adopting the kind of dispassionate, well-reasoned, "clearly articulated" method of arguing for "design propositions" that would lead to objective vocabularies free of personal bias.

Being a successful student, Manny suggested, required that a student, "had an implicit belief that what a teacher was professing was useful." Within the context of his "objective dialogue" teaching strategy, the better students were ones who made the "reversal" from talking about their work in the first person voice of the "I" to talking about their work in unbiased terms based on historical precedents, environmental factors, structural considerations, contextual determinants, or regulatory constraints. The better students could eventually develop the "poetic capacity" to clearly and precisely articulate conclusions they had reached through their process of objective reasoning. Students who resisted the "objective dialogue" approach might rise to the level of "technical competence," but they "probably" would not ascend into the level of acquiring the "poetic capacity" to produce designs reflective of the "ennobled qualities" of architecture.

Manny's vocabulary for narrating his experiences with his students, within which the construction of an objective dialogue was a central metaphor, implied a traditional theory of knowledge in several respects. As traditionally theorized, knowledge was objective, that is, it was thought to exist outside of subjective human experience. Genuine knowledge was traditionally thought to be separate in status from lower forms of biased opinions: higher level knowledge was not to be confused with lower level wants and likes. The mind's capacity for reason and dispassionate thought, the traditional theory suggested, enabled subjective data to be cleansed free of personal wants and likes. The sign of a reasoning, objective person, the old notion of knowledge concluded, was a capacity for clear verbal articulation of those discrete words and ideas that emerged at the end of the mind's opinion-cleansing operations.

Within Manny's narrative, his students' first steps toward acquisition of any valid knowledge about buildings, or neighborhoods, or cities, was to realize that real knowledge of architectural things was separate from what they "liked" about those things. Students who reacted spontaneously, who showed signs of responding based on their emotions, their gut reactions, their egos or identities, were engaging in behavior that was, as Manny termed it, "counter-productive" to their learning. In order to have real knowledge of what he called the "ennobled qualities" of architecture, his students would have to *separate* themselves *from* their *selves* by abandoning their immature habits of making descriptions that originated within the self, within "ego and identity." His student's thinking, reasoning, and persuasive argumentation capacities, Manny told me, "were signs of the intelligence of educated beings," and detachment from their subjective selves was their only recourse if they were to acquire *any* objective knowledge.

Following the traditional premise that higher knowledge was separate from lower level opinion, Manny believed that by separating their personal "likes" and "wants" from their design activities, students could control the discovery of objective design knowledge. In addition to using a "separation and control" type of metaphor to describe his students' processes of acquiring knowledge, Manny used that same type of metaphor to describe the relationship between himself (as a teacher) and his students (as learners). Manny told me that even though his "students were really desperate to know what he liked" he didn't "give away too much one way or another," meaning that he separated the person that he was from his teaching by intentionally excluding his own personal wants, or personal likes, from the "objective dialogue" conversations that he had with his students.

Except on rare occasions, he never let on as to whether he liked or disliked his students' designs based on personal reasons. In his teacher's role Manny acted the part of a detached observer, commenting on his students' work in terms of their reasoned arguments for their design propositions, which derived from their analytical responses to objective contextual criteria. Any hint that a building had derived its shape, its materials, its color, or its geometry from his students' personal "likes" or "wants" would be sniffed out as being personally biased and discarded as falling outside of the "objective dialogue" boundary that he had established. Separating his own personal criteria from the conversation with his students was part of his role as the agent who controlled the vocabulary that students were allowed to use within descriptions of their designs.

The traditional knowledge theory that appeared and reappeared in its various implied forms within Manny's narrative of his learning relationships with his students explained objective knowledge as existing outside of personal experience. This traditional theory was implicated within his description of the necessity of separating an objective vocabulary from a personal, first person "I" vocabulary for the sake of controlling the unwanted emergence of bias within his students' designs. In contrast to the metaphors of separation and control that implicated Manny's alignment with traditional theories of knowledge, Joe Constantino's metaphors of balance and connection pointed to a nontraditional set of premises in which the idea that students could discover an objective knowledge outside of their own first person encounters with their designs was abandoned, and replaced by the idea that knowledge was self-made entirely within personal experience.

Balance and Connection

Joe believed that the unique set of experiences, ideas, and intuitions that students brought to his studio, *along with* the vocabulary that they had developed for describing their personal inner lives, were the forces that drove their design processes. Joe had created a set of teaching practices in which he actively engaged in listening for his students' voices and vocabularies; a set of teaching practices in which students' descriptions of their wants and likes, spoken in the first person "I," were perceived as the source from which their "coherent overall project expressions" would emerge. He told me that one of the important messages that he felt needed to be conveyed to young designers was the importance of "balancing the intuitive with the rational and never losing track of one or the other." The "balancing intuition with rationality metaphor" for describing the design process that Joe used in describing his teaching approach pointed to his interest in validating his students' feelings and gut level responses as legitimate forms of wayfinding within the design process.

Joe's emphasis on sustaining the connection between the rational and intuitive derived from his understanding that losing one's sense of direction was a common occurrence within a process where there were no straight line paths to the final design solution.[2] Joe realized that intuitive starting points (a designer's first impressions about a site or about any other aspect of the design) often became the initial bases for later development of an "overall idea" that would ultimately enable the various parts of the building to be perceived as a whole. He understood how architects kept their descriptions of their intuitions in their peripheral awareness and brought them into the center of focus any time they found that they had lost their bearings and needed to regain a sense of direction, or needed to refocus the picture of a project's "overall coherence."

Within Joe's narrative of his interactions with his students he talked about his interest in having his students use their already acquired set of language capacities to make metaphors that referred to their intuitions. These metaphoric reference points could guide them toward the development of an architectural language of building forms that were reflective of the quality of "overall coherence" that their metaphors embodied. The role that the development of personal descriptions played in making intuitions useful was one of several roles that description-making played within his set of pedagogical practices. The process of making descriptions also pointed to Joe's definition of himself as a teacher, to his assumptions about his students as learners, and to his affinity with a nontraditional theory of knowledge. Language, within Joe's narrative of his conversations with students, was a tool for inventing personal descriptions of personal experiences. He understood that language *could not* exactly reflect intuitions because personal feelings and intuitions were so vague and indescribable to begin with. But this was a positive aspect of *both* language and intuition in that it pointed to *both* being susceptible to many equally valid interpretations.

For Joe, language was not a precision tool that could be used to hone in on one exact answer. Rather it was an interpretive tool that his students could use to test-out numerous descriptions of their design intuitions. Language was a way for his students to define their personal solutions without thinking that they would eventually arrive at a right or wrong solution. His students' metaphors, which they invented to mark their initial intuitions, became the personal standards by which they subsequently judged the merits of possible design moves related to building structure or budgetary constraints or other aspects of the rational phases of the design process.

Joe's message to students asserted the useful connection between intuition and rationality. His message to his students was that designing was a process in which designers attempted to "own and author" their own set of descriptions, and their own metaphors, by rationally and methodically testing out which of their numerous design alternatives could convey the kind of coherence that they intuitively felt at the beginning of the process. The kind of metaphor of connection that he used to describe the connection between intuition and rationality was also the kind of metaphor he used to describe his teacher's role as being connected with his students' roles in the design studio. As opposed to the traditional premise that the teacher-student learning relationship was based on the student learning the teacher's language, Joe's interaction with his students (which he called "co-designing") derived from his understanding that the architect's design talents were based on his or her capacity for concurrently speaking *both* an ordinary language that enabled the invention of personal metaphors and an unordinary language of building forms that enabled the creation of architectural designs.

The co-designing metaphor that Joe used to frame his learning relationship with his students implicated his abandonment of the idea that his teacher's knowledge (or teacher's vocabulary) was at a level separate from his students'. As opposed to the traditional conception that students were expected to adopt their teacher's language so that they could eventually replace their own lower level ordinary language with their teacher's higher level expert and extraordinary language, Joe's "co-designing" premise assumed that teacher and student were partners in a mutual learning process of giving and taking. By playfully transforming his students' ordinary language usage of words into an architectural language of building forms, Joe gave his students a set of architectural vocabulary options. This allowed his students to continually "own and author" their design ideas by choosing those pieces of Joe's architectural interpretations of their metaphors that fit into their personally defined directions, or by rejecting those pieces that missed the mark.

In listening for the emerging metaphors within his students' descriptions of their designs, Joe reflected an abandonment of the traditional conception that the teacher's true knowledge and expert language existed at a higher level separate from the student's lower level of opinion and ordinary language. Within Joe's "co-designing" set of teaching practices the teacher was free to interpret his students' metaphors in many different architectural ways, and the student was free to choose which pieces of their teacher's interpretation added strength to the foundation they had built. The price paid for the enjoyment of these pedagogical freedoms came by way of the nontraditional expectation that the teacher was expected to listen for the student's language, just as much as the student was expected to listen for the teacher's language.

Intuition and Rationality

Joe's practice of listening for his students' voices and vocabularies clearly contrasted with Manny's exclusion of student usage of language spoken in the first person "I." Manny believed that first person language signified opinion and emotion: aspects of language that, in Manny's perspective, were by definition not legitimate parts of the design process and not to be considered within dialogues aimed at the discovery of objective knowledge. The contrasts between Joe's and Manny's narratives about what counted or did not count as legitimate knowledge or legitimate vocabulary within their interactions with their students were useful in that they pointed to aspects of the traditional theory of knowledge (held by Manny) that Joe had implicitly abandoned, and the new theory Joe had adopted as the basis of his set of teaching practices.

The traditional theory of knowledge implicated in Manny's narrative suggested that since knowledge existed outside of experience, the discovery of real knowledge could occur only through detachment from the self, which was made possible by way of the mind's capacity for cold disinterest, logic, and reason. Opinion, emotion, intuition, interest, and bias, within the traditional definition of knowledge, were aspects of experience that were always suspect. These were bodily qualities that had to be constantly surveilled because they could lead to sabotaging the good work of the mind. Manny's interest in being the official in charge of controlling his students outcroppings of undesirable, biased, first person "I" vocabularies, pointed to the set of premises that underlay the traditional knowledge theory.

In contrast to Manny, Joe recognized that his students' first person "I" voices were indicators of their inner lives, their past experiences, and their sets of interests that would ultimately be expressed in their designs. All the vocabularies of all of his students counted. It was unnecessary for him to prohibit any of his students' ideas or ways of talking about their designs because Joe understood that his students' subjective voices, and their interests, intuitions, and biases, were the driving forces that kept their design investigations in focus. In contrast to Manny's emphasis on his students *separating* themselves *from* their selves, Joe emphasized that his students *connect* with their selves; connect with their intuitions, with their social concerns, with their interests in certain geometries, with anything personal that could become the basis for the central idea or the metaphoric proposition they needed to move their designs forward, toward a coherent consummation.[3]

As opposed to suspecting that his students' bodily modes of intelligence were saboteurs of the mind's capacities for rationality, Joe validated the necessary connection between body and mind within a design process where keeping the balance between intuition and rationality was of prime importance. As opposed to thinking that his students' knowledge needed to be objectified through detachment from personal history, biases, or interest, Joe understood that knowledge was self-made within a process in which self-made vocabularies became the points of contact between his students' personal experiences and their new experiences of learning to speak an architectural language. As opposed to posing himself as a teacher who knew what was best for his students, Joe listened for what his students thought was best for themselves as they described their own ways of thinking about, and their own sets of interests that drove, their work.

Joe's narrative use of a co-designing metaphor to describe his relationship to his students, and his use of a "balancing intuition with rationality" metaphor to portray his students' learning processes, have been characterized as a set of pedagogical metaphors of balance and connection. What has been presented here is the contrast between Joe's metaphors of balance and connection and the metaphors of separation and control that are reflective of Manny's set of teaching practices in which students separated themselves from their personal vocabularies in order to learn a set of objective approaches to designing. The contrast between their respective metaphors can also be interpreted as the contrast between educational practices built upon a traditional theory of knowledge and an alternative set of teaching practices driven by a new set of premises about knowledge. The metaphors of self that Gina Vismara used in framing her narrative descriptions of learning relationships with students were an additional perspective that thickened the layers of descriptive differences between old and new teaching practices based on traditional and alternative conceptions of knowledge.

Metaphors of Inner Self

Within the narrative of her experiences in the beginning design studio, Gina emphasized her interest in "nurturing" her students' capacities for "working independently" by validating and supporting their inventions of their own original vocabularies for talking about, and making, their designs. She told me that she looked for moments when her students would argue for their designs based on their own ideas. These "moments of conviction," as she called them, were indicators that a student's "designer's personality" was beginning to emerge. Gina told me that students undergoing their initial design studio experiences tended to have a "very hard time abandoning convention" because they were afraid of "taking the risk" of being different. Influenced by magazines, previous teachers, as well as their design studio peers, students tended to drop their own original ideas in favor of safer sets of architectural conventions and norms. She saw her role as a teacher in terms of the support she could give to her students as they learned to "let go" of the conventions of normal architectural language. By coming to what she called "an awareness" of their "personal or inner selves," students could step outside of the existing set of architectural norms and create vocabularies of building form that were as unique as they themselves were.

Gina believed that by "manipulating" the conventions of existing architectural language, students could eventually gain the confidence needed to develop their own original vocabularies. That confidence and commitment to their own ideas and architectural vocabularies would come at the same time that they gained insight into their own unique sets of inner qualities: qualities of the personal self that she defined as the core of the "designer's personality." Gina's set of teaching strategies was based on her interest in having her students learn to recognize their own evolving "designer's personality" by making use of their unique personal interests and cultural backgrounds within their designs.

Recall that Julia, one of Gina's students, was, at one point in her design exploration, developing an architectural vocabulary of form based on the "flickering candle" metaphor that had emerged from her personal interest in the spatial experiences of light and shadow. Or Ernesto, whose Latino cultural background pointed him toward an exploration of Mexican architect Luis Barragan's exterior façade color schemes. Because she believed that any form of vocabulary that was expressive of the self could lead to breaking away from the existing conventions of architectural form making, Gina validated and supported her students' design explorations in which they invented vocabularies based on their unique experiences, on their cultural identities, or on various other aspects of their personal selves.

The "awareness of inner self" metaphor that Gina used in narrating her students' process of developing their personal sets of architectural vocabularies reflected her belief that the language her students used to describe their designs was *not separate* from the language they used to describe themselves: that their descriptions of their designs could derive from descriptions that reflected their awareness of their personal interests, their unique wants, and their cultural roots. Within the narrative of her interactions with students, Gina talked about her students' processes of learning to design in terms of their "ability to translate metaphor kinds of concepts into spaces." She believed that if their metaphors emerged from their personal backgrounds, idiosyncratic interests, or cultural heritage, then her students' metaphors could bridge their identities as persons with their identities as architects.

Julia's fascination with translucent light, which motivated her invention of a metaphor in which space was likened to a "flickering candle"; Kenny's "unstable room" metaphor for visual contradiction, which had its origins in his childhood memories of "a dark, scary closet"; and Irv's intrigue with medieval monasteries, which led to his "urban monastery" metaphor for the development of a hotel in downtown San Francisco; were all examples of the kinds of metaphoric starting points within her students' processes of translating language into building forms. Gina's message to her students was that metaphors that emerged from the self and eventually resulted in architectural translations into building form were metaphors that pointed to the intimacy between the thing created and its creator; between designs created and the designer's self.

Knowledge Awaiting Discovery

Gina's validation of her students' personal voices was meant to point them toward limiting their dependencies on external architectural norms and conventions. She believed that as her students gradually shifted their search for design ideas away from magazines, or peer pressure, or other external sources, and toward their own backgrounds, idiosyncrasies, memories, even their phobias, they would gain confidence in their abilities to work independently: they would drop their habit of depending on external factors as they gradually picked up on "an awareness of their inner selves." The "awareness of inner self metaphor" that Gina used to frame her interaction with her students implicated her interest in abandoning the traditional theory that knowledge existed outside of the self. In contrast to Manny, who framed his students' habitual reliance on their internal sets of motivating forces as detriments to the learning process, Gina understood the detriments to learning in terms of her students' habitual reliance on external sets of conventional architectural stimuli.

The difference in viewpoints, in this case, pointed to one example of the difference between what learning meant within the context of educational theories and practices founded on an old knowledge theory *and* what learning meant to teachers who showed an interest in adopting new sets of practices based on a nontraditional theory of knowledge. In Manny's case, following the old theory, learning was a process that required detachment from the self, in that learning was the acquisition of objective knowledge that existed outside of personal experience. This did not mean that his students could not gain knowledge of design issues because they had subjective experiences, emotions, ideas, desires, or preferences. What it did mean was that if they were to acquire knowledge of which of their ideas were objectively true and which were biased by their own subjectivity, then they would have to deploy a method by which they could be independent of their subjectivity.

Manny's teaching approach was based on teaching students various methods of separating their selves from their selves because he believed that legitimate knowledge was of the kind that existed independent of his student's subjectivity. His objectifying methodologies included analytical considerations of objective contextual determinants, studies of historic precedent, and exclusion of first person vocabularies from argumentation. Learning, following traditional theory, was a process of effectively using reliable methods for discovering knowledge outside of the self. In contrast, Gina's view of her students' learning processes was framed within the perspective that knowledge was something that already existed within her students' personal experiences. Her narrative descriptions of her interactions with students implicated her attempt at an *abandonment* of the idea that her students' knowledge existed outside of their inner selves. In thinking that knowledge already existed within her students' inner selves Gina thought about learning in terms of its internal origins.

A student like Catherine, who turned to magazines or historic precedents as starting points in her design explorations, was problematic within Gina's point of view because the turn to external rather than internal sources of knowledge was a sign of Catherine's absence of "conviction to her work"; an absence of an "awareness of the self." Manny, on the other hand, might have enthusiastically endorsed Catherine's turn toward a set of external sources of design exploration based on his interest in having his students drop their immature dependence on internal likes and dislikes. The "reverse image" set of objections found in Manny's objection to the *internal* origins of illegitimate subjective knowledge as compared to Gina's objection to the *external* origins of impersonal knowledge, pointed to an aspect of defining knowledge that Manny and Gina held in common: that knowledge preexisted somewhere, in some form, waiting to be discovered.

Their shared conception of knowledge as definable in terms of its preexisting location was useful because it pointed to a view often held by teachers who, like Gina, believed that an emphasis on their students' internal interests and personalities signified abandonment of the conventional view that knowledge preexisted outside of the self. But by replacing the concept that the locus of knowledge was external with the concept that the locus of knowledge was internal, Gina only went halfway toward making a clean break from past traditions because she still held that knowledge had a place of residence, an address that could be found no matter how far into the self one had to delve. Gina's conception of knowledge differed from Manny's in the sense that the journey toward the discovery of knowledge would take her students into the deep recesses of the self, whereas the journey toward the discovery of knowledge that Manny's students embarked on might take them into the outer stratospheres beyond the self. But in either case, knowledge was discovered, it was preexisting, and it had locatable origins.

Problematic students, in both Gina's and Manny's narratives, were those whose personal vocabularies for talking about their design works did not align with their own (teachers') conception of the best method for *discovering* knowledge. In Manny's case, students whose descriptions of their work pointed toward intelligence modes of the bodily, intuitive, or interpersonal sort, were students viewed as having had less capacity than those whose vocabularies depicted their bent toward logic, or reason, or objective deduction.[4] In Gina's case, students whose design vocabularies were based in external or material sources outside of their inner selves, were students thought to have less capacity than those whose metaphors originated in their personal backgrounds or interests. Within both sets of narratives related to their studio experiences, certain of their students' vocabularies were approved, others disapproved.

Gina remained within the same theoretical circle that Manny occupied by *inverting* rather *abandoning* the position that knowledge preexisted, awaiting discovery. While Gina's "metaphors of self," compared to Manny's "metaphors of separation and control," pointed toward the various differences in their approaches to defining knowledge, teaching, and learning, her underlying assumption that knowledge was discovered led her to think that students whose interests or vocabularies *did not* point toward their "awareness of the self" were less capable of discovering knowledge compared to those students whose expressive modes were oriented toward self-discovery. Contrasting both Gina's "metaphors of self" and Manny's "metaphors of separation and control" with Joe's "metaphors of balance and connection" was useful in that it pointed to ways in which Joe's reflections on his set of teaching practices implicated his abandonment of traditional knowledge theory.

Knowledge Emerged

Joe's narrative of his interactions with students pointed to his having abandoned the idea that knowledge was discovered and having replaced it with the understanding that his students made knowledge as they made descriptions of their sets of design process experiences. Joe's narrative implicated his understanding that there was no need to think in terms of a "best" method for discovering knowledge because knowledge was not something that existed *before* it was made. Joe understood his students' design explorations as processes in which they were unable to have knowledge of what it was that they intended to do before they developed the language that made it possible for them to articulate what they had done. Or put another way, Joe understood that his students did not have immediate knowledge of their designs, but rather their knowledge emerged as they began to invent ways of describing those parts of their experiences that they had already undergone.

For example, Joe did not assume that in making exploratory models of their work that his students were "discovering" historic architectural precedent, or "discovering their inner selves." Instead he assumed that within the process of model making, each of their design moves would lead to many descriptions that in retrospect could help explain what had happened during that time that they were making those design moves. Recall that the vocabulary that Roberto had applied to his cultural arts center design (after he had gone through several model explorations) made it possible for the first time for him to have knowledge that his "theater spaces" were "volumes" and his "hallways and exterior walls" were "planes." Roberto did not have the knowledge that his design was about "volumes" and "planes" until he made up a vocabulary to describe his process of exploring his design. The making of the "volumes and planes" vocabulary was the making of the knowledge he came to have about his design.

In abandoning the idea that his students' knowledge preexisted, and replacing it with the understanding that their knowledge emerged as they retrospectively made descriptions of their sets of design explorations, Joe focused his set of teaching practices on listening for his students' descriptions of their work as they saw it and spoke it through their sets of eyes and their sets of vocabularies. Joe shared with Gina the pedagogical commitment that learning began with the interests of the learner but because he had dropped the idea that the learner's knowledge preexisted, the problem of defining whose method of discovering knowledge was most adequate did not emerge within his experiences with his students (as it did in Gina's experience with her students). Joe and Gina also shared an interest in their students making linguistic metaphors that would inform their making of architectural vocabularies of form. But instead of seeing their metaphor making as a reflection of a *discovery* of some part of their inner selves, Joe understood that their making of metaphors *was* their making of their selves: that by making descriptions of their design explorations they were making descriptions of the designer that they had become during their individual processes of exploration.

In dropping the idea that knowledge was a discovered thing, there was no need for Joe to think that his architect's vocabulary entitled him to an inherently truer, or better, or larger knowledge of architecture as compared to his students.   Joe recognized the difference between his students' ordinary spoken language and his architectural language as a difference between the roles that each of these languages played within one process (the design process), not a difference in their legitimacy within the process. He understood that ordinary language, within the design process, was useful in the development of linguistic metaphors, *and* that architectural language was useful in the development of building forms.

Because Joe understood that architects spoke both languages concurrently, he did not pose himself as a teacher whose language was to be imitated, but rather as a teacher who exemplified the architect's process of going back and forth between languages on the way to authoring his or her own design solution. Students felt that they had the choice of accepting or rejecting any of the expert architectural vocabulary that Joe used to talk about their work because he consistently posed *his* vocabulary in terms of its applicability (or non-applicability) to the metaphors that *they* had authored. Within a mutual process in which teacher and student co-authored an interactive design inquiry, the artificial border between teacher and student dissolved, students retained authorship of their design works, and Joe retained authorship of his way of teaching.

Vocabularies Brought to Life

Within Joe's, Gina's, and Manny's respective narrations of their design studio experiences with their students, there emerged a set of metaphors that alluded to each of their perspectives about themselves as teachers and each of their views about their relationship to students' learning processes. In an attempt to understand their pedagogical perspectives within a wider historical context, the theory of knowledge that each of their narratives implicated has been pointed to and discussed at length. Their metaphors could be taken as a set of starting points for future conversations about educational practice and theory. Others have already pointed to a possible set of starting points that were, in many ways, similar to the set that emerged within this investigation.

The usefulness of the kinds of listening practices that enabled Joe to hear the multiple vocabularies of his students as spoken from their perspectives (which enabled them to retain "ownership" of their designs) has been explored by Mike Martin, who wrote about listening for students' voices and vocabularies within design studio pedagogy in terms of "personalizing skills." Martin wrote:

> The skills of taking alternative frames of reference play a major part in personalizing a human situation. These alternative frames of reference allow the opportunity to view the human situation from many differing perspectives, thus providing more thoughtful, accurate, and constructive insights into the process of exploring and understanding the human situation by the participants... As a result of personalizing, personal ownership of where a person is in relationship to where he or she wants to be is attained. This personal ownership represents the first step in initiating a set of strategies for acting on the goals of the participant.[5]

Gina's interest in the development of pedagogy that focused on the "discovery of the inner self" within the act of designing has been explored by Stefani Ledewitz, who pointed to the role of discovery and insight within the design process, writing,

> Design is not commonly thought of as a discovery process. In part, this is because the outcome is not what is traditionally thought of as knowledge, but rather, "insights." These insights may concern the nature of the design problem... they may concern the design process... or they may concern the designer himself... Insightful knowledge, or "seeing into" the problem is a "grasp of things that goes deeper than words." It is tacit, or in Polanyi's terms, "personal knowledge" that we cannot make explicit... Design differs from other learning experiences not only in the kind of knowledge it produces, but also in the process of discovery itself.[6]

Manny's type of "construction of an objective dialogue" within the design studio has been explored by Amos Rapoport, who similarly mistrusts "personal and subjective" intrusions within educative processes of learning to design. Rapoport wrote:

In setting explicit objectives for design, criteria are also set for evaluating how successfully goals have been met. When this process is repeated, there is hope of developing a cumulative body of knowledge and theory... It seems self-evident that both design goals and criteria of evaluation are always necessarily related to, and dependent on a theory; one needs first to know what built environments can do before one can assess whether any given specimen does it well or badly. Yet there is no valid theory of design involved in the teaching of design worth that name. Without such a theory, design cannot be taught and is not really suitable as a university subject. Its approach is personal, subjective, illogical and not cumulative.[7]

Joe's, Gina's, and Manny's respective narrations of their experiences with their students, within which their set of metaphors for teaching emerged, have been analyzed in a way that, as I described earlier, is itself metaphorical (in the sense that each of their narratives were analyzed in terms of the two other teachers' vocabularies). At this point in the study, if we followed the traditional option we would equate further analysis with the search for whether Joe's metaphors of balance and connection were better than Gina's metaphors of self, or whether Manny's metaphors of separation and control were better than Joe's metaphors of balance and connection, and so on. Following traditional forms of analysis we could compare the studies of those researchers that I have mentioned above (each of whom alluded to one of the three metaphors being studied here) in terms of which of these researchers' positions was the most accurate representation of a studio type of education, or which of them most effectively described a best model for teaching.

Alternatively, recognizing that educational practice vocabularies that emerged within this study would someday be replaced by new vocabularies that supported new sets of teaching practices, we would use the metaphorical analysis presented in this chapter to look *for beginnings* rather than conclusions. In the conversation that we engaged in with our colleagues, each of whom (including ourselves) might have a favorite metaphor (a favorite perspective on education), we would listen *for the beginnings* of new metaphors. By accepting that metaphors brought into the conversation were neither right or wrong, but rather were just various versions, various descriptions, of an event (the event of teaching our students) that we all felt was worth talking about, we would listen for those new hybrid combinations, or new mutations, or new derivations, or new connections, that might have emerged as the metaphors that we each brought into the conversation collided into, or connected with, or transformed as a result of their intersection with, those metaphors that our colleagues brought with them.

Following the modern poet, if we accepted the transience of metaphor without thinking that the cyclicity of new metaphors replacing old ones was part of a process of searching for and finding new vocabularies that could bring us that much closer to the Truth, we might begin to rethink the usefulness of the inevitable lives and deaths of educational practice metaphors. Abandoning our habit of thinking that new disciplinary vocabularies emerged because a community of practitioners had discovered the old vocabulary to be flawed and the new one to be the real Truth, would require an abandonment of the idea that Truth existed outside of human descriptions of it. To abandon the idea that Truth and Knowledge were discovered would lead us to think, for example, that the statement that "The earth is a sphere," did not bring seventeenth century astronomers any closer to the Truth than the statement made by their predecessors that, "The earth was flat."

Such a thought *would not* require that we think that the sentence "The earth is a sphere," was not true. Alternatively, adopting the perspective that knowledge and truth were human inventions would point us in the direction of understanding that the sentence, "The earth is a sphere," *was true* for its seventeenth century users, not because it corresponded to an antecedently existing timeless Truth, but because its speakers, its inventors, had gotten so used to speaking it, so confident in its capacity to guide their everyday practices, so habituated to the sound of it and the thought of it, that they had come to believe and act *as if* it were true.

Within this alternative perspective, truth and knowledge would be understood to be humanly made within human experience. The shift from the use of a "flat earth" metaphor to the use of a "spherical earth" metaphor, which happened within the astronomic community between the hundred year period that separated Copernicus and Galileo, would then be understood as part of process in which old metaphors inevitably broke down and newly invented metaphors inevitably replaced them. Recognizing the inevitable "impermanence of metaphor" could help us see seventeenth century astronomers as being one example of a community of practitioners who eventually dropped one vocabulary for another over the long period of time that it took for them to get used to speaking and thinking about their work, and their world, in new ways.

With the modern poet's *metaphoric impermanence* perspective of the new "spherical earth" vocabulary in mind, we might decide to stop thinking that our time spent plowing through astronomic proofs of a heliocentric solar system could eventually result in our finding out how seventeenth century astronomers went about discovering truth. Rather, we might begin thinking of seventeenth century astronomic publications as one of many genres of literature that emerged during that era.[8] If we abandoned the idea that truth awaited seventeenth-century astronomers, we might alternatively start understanding that their process of transitioning from talking about a "flat earth" to talking about a "spherical earth" occurred within a process in which they gradually become used to using a new astronomic vocabulary that aligned and connected with the set of ideas and vocabularies that practitioners within many disciplines were beginning to adopt at that particular moment in history. We might then attempt to understand how seventeenth century astronomic metaphors were influenced by seeds of ideas that could have floated from within the landscape of numerous other practice communities and onto the soil that astronomers tilled.

It might, at that point, become possible to think that the sets of metaphors that we use as shorthand abbreviations for the guiding premises behind practices at the heart of the architectural discipline could be influenced by new ideas that have floated from other disciplines into the world of architecture. Architects might then feel at ease with borrowing ideas and vocabularies from outside the field of architecture and architectural education, and not be as concerned with practitioners from other disciplines who freely borrow architectural ideas and vocabularies. And this might move architects toward entertaining the possibility that their students were more interested in borrowing traditional architectural vocabulary for their own uses than they were in the wholesale adoption of a way of thinking, speaking, and designing that was *not* their own. Those of us in "academic" teaching roles might learn from William James, who put the "mutual borrowing" between disciplines in terms of "the younger generation" being *less* interested in adopting "academic" ideas, and *more* interested in listening for those new ideas that resonated with their own experiences of "the temperament of life." James wrote,

> It is difficult not to notice a curious unrest in the philosophic atmosphere of the time, a loosening of old landmarks, a softening of oppositions, a mutual borrowing from one another on the part of systems anciently closed, and an interest in new suggestions, however vague, as if one thing sure were the inadequacy of the extant school-solutions. The dissatisfaction with these seems due for the most part to a feeling that they are too abstract and academic. Life is confused and

superabundant, and what the younger generation appears to crave is more of the temperament of life in its philosophy, even tho it were at some cost of logical rigor and of formal purity.[9]

Following James, it would be difficult for architectural educators not to notice the difference between the predominant architectural use of the term "postmodern" as a metaphoric shorthand for defining that set of late twentieth century stylistic conventions that replaced the Modern architect's set of "form follows function" aesthetic canons *and* its predominant usage (that evolved after it was borrowed from architectural discourse) within philosophical and literary criticism discourses. For philosophers and literary critics, the term "postmodern" has become shorthand for the abandonment of the long-held idea that truth and knowledge about the inherent order of the world could be discovered. "Postmodern," in its architectural context, in the early 1970s, referred to the method of discovering the "order" within certain kinds of "ordinary" buildings that were distinctly *not* Modern. By the late 1970s, "postmodern" became the new vocabulary of architectural form making that announced itself as having rendered the old Modern "functionalist" vocabulary obsolete.[10]

The architects who pioneered "postmodern architecture" took it for granted that periodic shifts within the discipline were the result of someone having found a truer set of premises for thinking about, or someone having discovered a better method for producing, architecture. In contrast, the postmodern philosopher's and literary theorist's understanding was that periodic disciplinary shifts in thought and speech pointed to the inevitable phenomenon in which, over long periods of time, certain ideas and vocabularies caught on, while others diminished in popularity. Unlike the late twentieth century architect, the postmodern philosopher and literary critic did not think that the rise of the usage of one metaphor (during a given historic era) that coincided with the fall of another metaphor was a sign of the risen vocabulary's superiority compared to the other's inferiority. For philosopher and literary theorist, both the rise and fall of metaphors during particular historic eras would be examples of the inevitability of what Robert Frost called the "break down" of all metaphor.

The distinction between the architect's use of the term "postmodern" and the use that philosophers and literary critics have made of it can be understood as a difference between the old idea that knowledge and truth are found and the new idea that knowledge and truth are made. The new sets of ideas embodied within the poet's and philosopher's new version of "postmodern" (a transformation of the architect's old version) might be reflective of ideas "craved" by those architecture students who comprise today's "younger generation." The "younger generation" of architecture students, in other words, might be less interested in the architectural version of "postmodern," which supported the idea that designers could discover the inherent truth within designed objects, or the inherent truth within themselves as they engaged in the process of designing, and more interested in the poets and philosophers who abandoned the old idea that acts of creation amounted to discovering inherent truths, and adopted the understanding that acts of creation were acts of creating one's self.[11]

Perhaps architecture students (like other students), as James suspected, "crave more of the temperament of life in *its* philosophy," not in their teacher's philosophy. Perhaps the message that truths and philosophies are human inventions, a message being conveyed to our younger generation within the songs and poems created by the current crop of poets *and* within the films and writings of the current crop of philosophers, is a message that they bring with them to the design studio in the form of their voices and their vocabularies.[12] Perhaps listening for our students could be understood as a way of concurrently validating who they have become within their interactions with us and who we have become within the interactions we have had with them.

Of course we could continue to follow the traditional notion that we teachers have the privilege and power to validate or invalidate our students' vocabularies. We could continue responding to those students whose vocabularies contradict our own by insisting that they are inadequate, uninformed, more conventional, or less insightful, as compared to our teacher's vocabulary. Or, alternatively, we could entertain the possibility that occasions when we found ourselves resisting our students' voices and vocabularies could become opportunities for us to examine whether our own perspectives might be informed by theirs. We might also see as a possibility that listening to our students' explanations of the metaphors that we find dissonant with our own could add to our understanding of who they are and what sets of personal experiences drive their descriptions of the world.

Finally, if we could ever step beyond the shadow of our Greek and Cartesian ancestors' urgency for finding everlasting truth, and bring ourselves to commit to dropping our habit of resolving occasions of metaphoric dissonance by determining whose description was the best of the bunch, we might find that some of our students' manipulations of our old vocabularies have resulted in the making of metaphors fresh with the energy that ours used to embody; and that realization might make us wonder if our habitual ways of thinking and talking about the world have outlived their usefulness, and in the end that might just lead us to changing, or perhaps abandoning, our dead or dying vocabularies and adopting some new description that one of our students has brought to life.

Notes

Chapter One: Vocabularies Collided

1   See Owen Gingerich, *The Great Copernicus Chase and Other Adventures in Astronomical History* (Cambridge, MA: Sky Publications Corporation; Cambridge [England]: Cambridge University Press, 1992) p. 32.

2   See Thomas S. Kuhn, *The Copernican Revolution: Planetary Astronomy in the Development of Western Thought* (Cambridge, MA: Harvard University Press, 1957).

3   See Galileo Galilei, *Dialogue Concerning the Two Chief World Systems,* translated by Stillman Drake (Berkeley: University of California Press, 1953).

4   See Thomas Kuhn, *The Structure of Scientific Revolutions, 2nd ed.* (Chicago: University of Chicago Press, 1970).

5   See Richard Rorty, *Contingency, irony, and solidarity* (New York: Cambridge University Press, 1989) p. 6.

6   The issue of scientific method and its role in the discovery of knowledge has been discussed at length by various authors. See, for example, Karl Popper, *The Logic of Scientific Discovery* (New York: Routledge, 1992); Larry Laudan, *Science and Relativism: Some Key Controversies in the Philosophy of Science* (Chicago: University of Chicago Press, 1990); Israel Scheffler, *Science and Subjectivity* (Indianapolis: Hackett Publishing Co., 1982); Arthur Holly Compton, *The Human Meaning of Science* (Chapel Hill: University of North Carolina Press, 1940).

7   In his investigation of issues of objectivity and the admittance of fact into scientific bodies of knowledge, Bernard Williams writes, "if knowledge is what it claims to be, then it is knowledge of a reality which exists independently of that knowledge, and... independently of any thought or experience." This independence does not mean that knowledge cannot be discovered by individuals who have subjective emotions, ideas, memories, desires, prejudices, commitments or beliefs. What this does mean for Williams is that the truth or falsity of a knowledge claim is totally independent of the particular set of inner motives that an individual possesses. See Bernard Williams, *Descartes: The Project of Pure Inquiry* (Atlantic Highlands, NJ: Humanities Press, 1978) p. 64. Examples of other works in which authors examine the role of scientific

testing in the discovery of objective knowledge include John Searle, *The Rediscovery of the Mind* (Cambridge, MA: MIT Press, 1992); Karl Popper, *Conjecture and Refutation* (New York: Basic Books, 1962); Ernest Nagel, Sylvain Bromberger and Adolf Grunbaum, *Observation and Theory in Science* (Baltimore: Johns Hopkins University Press, 1971); Harold I. Brown, *Rationality* (New York: Routledge, 1988).

8   See Richard Rorty, *Philosophy and the Mirror of Nature* (Princeton: Princeton University Press, 1990).

9   John Searle reviews the features of what he calls the "Western Rationalistic Tradition," that started with Aristotle and other Greek philosophers. For Searle the scientific tradition of objectivity is at the heart of the "rationalistic tradition." He emphasizes this point, writing "If someone makes a claim to truth and can give that claim the right kind of support, and if that claim is indeed true, then that person genuinely knows something. The fact that the whole enterprise of claiming and validating may have been carried out by someone who is racist or sexist is just irrelevant to the truth of the claim. This is part of what is meant by saying that knowledge is objective." See John R. Searle, "Rationality and Realism, What is at Stake?," *Daedalus* 122 (Fall 1993): 66–67.

10 For a review of Descartes' attempted resolution of the paradox between images of the mind and materials in the world see Roger Ariew and Marjorie Grene (eds.), *Descartes and His Contemporaries: Meditations, Objections, and Replies* (Chicago: University of Chicago Press, 1995).

11 The interest in the metaphor "mind as machine," that began with Descartes, continues today in much of the research within the cognitive science community. For texts that explore the modern argument that machines can operate in much the same way that the mind does, see, for example: A. M. Turing, "Can a Machine Think?," in *The World of Mathematics,* James R. Newman, ed. (New York: Simon and Schuster, 1956), pp. 2099–2123; Marvin Minsky, *The Society of Mind* (New York: Simon and Schuster, 1986); Daniel Dennett, *Consciousness Explained* (Boston: Little, Brown and Company, 1991).

12 For an interesting discussion of the influence that Descartes' set of epistemological assumptions have had on the contemporary theory about the bodily aspect of experience (emotion, intuition, etc.) see (especially the introduction) Allison M. Jagger and Susan R. Bordo, eds., *Gender/Body/Knowledge* (New Brunswick, NJ: Rutgers University Press, 1989).

13 See Charles Darwin, *On the Origins of Species by Means of Natural Selection* (London: John Murry, 1859).

14 See John Dewey, *The Influence of Darwin on Philosophy* (New York: Holt and Company, 1910), pp. 11–12.

15 See John Dewey, *How We Think: A Restatement of the Relation of Reflective Thinking to the Educative Process* (Boston: Heath, 1933).

16 See, for example, Clarence Irving Lewis, "The Knowledge of Objects," in *Mind and the World-Order* (NY: Dover, 1929), pp. 117–153; Jacques Derrida, "Structure, Sign, and Play in the Discourse of the Human Sciences." *Writing and Difference,* trans. by Alan Bass (Chicago: University of Chicago Press, 1978), pp. 287–293; Richard Rorty, *Objectivity, relativism, and truth* (New York: Cambridge University Press, 1991); Hilary Putnam, *Realism and Reason* (Cambridge [England]: Cambridge University Press, 1983).

17 See, for example, William Heard Kilpatrick, *Foundations of Method: Informal Talks on Teaching* (New York: The Macmillan Company, 1925); Harold Rugg, *Culture and Education in America* (New York: Harcourt, Brace and Company, 1931); John L. Childs, *Education and Morals: An Experimentalist Philosophy of Education* (New York: Appleton-Century-Crofts, Inc., 1950); Walter Feinberg and Jonas F. Soltis, *School and Society* (New York: Teachers College Press, 1985).

18 Hillary Putnam challenges the Greek/Cartesian idea that human objectivity can be gained through detachment, which he refers to as the idea that through certain methodologies humans could have a "God's eye view" of reality. See Hilary Putnam, *Realism with a Human Face* (Cambridge, MA: Harvard University Press, 1990). Also see Elisabeth A. Lloyd, "Objectivity and the Double Standard for Feminist Epistemologies," *Synthese* 104 (1995):351–381; Hayden White, "The Value of Narrativity in the Representation of Reality," in *The Content of the Form* (Baltimore: Johns Hopkins University Press, 1987), pp. 1–25; Michel Foucault, *The History of Sexuality,* trans. by Robert Hurley (New York: Vintage Press, 1978).

19 See John Dewey, "Philosophy," Edwin R. A. Seligman, ed., *Encyclopedia of the Social Sciences, Vol. II* (New York: Macmillan Company, 1962), 128. For the exploration of the Deweyan idea that imaginative ventures are valid without claiming objective truth, see Nelson Goodman, *Ways of Worldmaking* (Indianapolis: Hackett Press, 1978); Elliot W. Eisner, *The Enlightened Eye: Qualitative Inquiry and the Enhancement of Educational Practice* (New York: Macmillan Publishing Co., 1991); Susanne K. Langer, *Mind: An Essay on Human Feeling, Vol. 1* (Baltimore: Johns Hopkins University Press, 1976).

20 For a background introduction to educational projects undertaken by "speakers of the *discovered knowledge* vocabulary," see Robert Westbrook's discussion of progressive educators' various interests and projects that related to the "social potentialities" of education in his *John Dewey and American Democracy* (Ithaca, NY: Cornell University Press, 1991), 500–510.

Chapter Two: Theorizing Knowledge

1   For the history of the relationship between poetic and philosophical theories of various eras see Mark Edmundson, *Literature Against Philosophy: From Plato to Derrida, a Defense of Poetry* (Cambridge [England]: Cambridge University Press, 1995).

2   For a discussion of the Romantic and the Modern poet's abandonment of the "discovered knowledge" thesis see Richard Rorty, "The Contingency of Language," *Contingency, irony, and solidarity* (New York: Cambridge University Press, 1989), 6.

3   Richard Rorty frames this point about society selecting certain metaphors by chance, writing "the difference between genius and fantasy is not the difference between impresses that lock on to something universal, some antecedent reality out there in the world or deep within the self, and those that do not. Rather, it is the difference between idiosyncrasies which just happen to catch on with other people—happen because of the contingencies of some historical situation, some particular need which a given community happens to have at a given time." See his *Contingency, irony, and solidarity*, 37.

4   Robert Frost, "Mending Wall," in *North of Boston*, (London: D. Nutt, 1914).

5   John Dewey, *Art as Experience* (New York: Perigee Books, 1980), 35.

6   Dewey explores cosmological conceptions from the Greek era to the early twentieth century in his *Quest for Certainty, John Dewey: The Later Works, 1925–1958 Vol. 12: 1938*, ed. Jo Ann Boydston (Carbondale, IL: Southern Illinois University Press, 1991).

7   See John Dewey, *Experience and Nature* (New York: Dover Publications, Inc., 1958), 86.

8   See Mark Johnson, "On the Nature of Meaning," *The Body in the Mind, The Bodily Basis of Meaning, Imagination and Reason* (Chicago: University of Chicago Press, 1987), 177.

9   See, for example, Susan Bordo, *Unbearable Weight: Feminism, Western Culture, and the Body* (Berkeley: University of California Press, 1993); Linda Brodkey and Michelle Fine, "Presence of Mind in the Absence of Body," *Journal of Education [Boston University]* 170 (1988): 84–99.

10   Thomas Barone, "Breaking the Mold: The New American Student as Strong Poet," *Theory Into Practice* 32 (Autumn 1993): 239.

11   Barone, *Theory Into Practice*, 238.

12 Donald A. Schön, *Educating the Reflective Practitioner* (San Francisco: Jossey-Bass Publishers, 1987) pp. 94–95. In the text from which I quote, the interchange that the author describes is between a male professor and a female student, so I have changed the gender in the quote from the "he" in the original text to "she" in this text.

13 Schön, "The Architectural Studio as an Exemplar of Education for Reflection-in-Action," *Journal of Architectural Education* 38 (Fall 1984): 7.

14 Mike Martin describes what I refer to as the process of "listening for the conflicts that emerge as different voices intersect," as "an empathic understanding of discrepancy." He writes, "If the situation is a human situation, as is almost always the case in architecture... then the act of design could be defined as the process of establishing the content, feelings, meanings, problems, and goals of the observed discrepancy. This requires both a logical and a reasoned way of 'knowing' in addition to a subjective way of 'knowing.' These ways of 'knowing' can provide an empathic understanding of the discrepancy. Thus, a plan of action to resolve the discrepancy can be formulated through the personal ownership of the human situation." See Martin's "A Beginning Course in Environmental Design: A Humanist Approach," *Fostering Creativity in Architectural Education, Proceedings of the ACSA West Central Conference* (conference held at University of Illinois at Urbana-Champagne, 1986).

15 Carol Gilligan, Lyn Mikel Brown, and Annie G. Rogers, "The Psyche Embedded: A Place for Body, Relationships, and Culture in Personality Theory" (Monograph #4, Harvard University Laboratory of Human Development, 1988) p. 6.

16 Richard Coyne and Adrian Snodgrass, "Is designing mysterious? challenging the dual knowledge thesis." *Design Studies* 12 (July 1991): 128.

17 Coyne and Snodgrass, *Design Studies*, 130–131.

18 Coyne and Snodgrass, *Design Studies*, 130–131.

Chapter Three: Metaphor and Methodology

1 See Robert Frost, "Education by Poetry," in *Selected Prose of Robert Frost*, eds. Hyde Cox and Edward Connery Lathem (San Francisco: Holt, Reinhart and Winston, 1966) pp. 33–46.

2 Elliot Eisner, "On the Differences between Scientific and Artistic Approaches to Qualitative Research," *Educational Researcher* 10 (April 1981): 6.

3   See Robert Coles, "On the Nature of Character: Some Preliminary Field Notes," *Daedalus* 110 (Fall 1981): 131–143; Philip W. Jackson, "Secondary Schooling for Children of the Poor," "Comprehending a Well-Run Comprehensive: A Report on a Visit to a Large Suburban High School," and "Secondary Schooling for the Privileged Few: A Report on a Visit to a New England Boarding School," *Daedalus* 110(Fall 1981): 39–57, 81–95, and 117–130; Sara Lawrence-Lightfoot, "Portraits of Exemplary Secondary Schools: George Washington Carver Comprehensive School," "Portraits of Exemplary Secondary Schools: Highland Park," and "Portraits of Exemplary Secondary Schools: St. Paul's School," *Daedalus* 110 (Fall 1981): 17–37, 59–80, 97–116.

4   See Jonathan Kozol, *Death at an Early Age; The Destruction of the Hearts and Minds of Negro Children in the Boston Public Schools* (New York: Bantam Press, 1968).

5   See Vivian Gussin Paley, *White Teacher* (Cambridge, MA: Harvard University Press, 1979).

6   See Roland S. Barth, *Run School Run* (Cambridge, MA: Harvard University Press, 1980).

7   While most qualitative researchers share a commitment to engaging in the type of investigation where "evidence" is conveyed through description rather than "statistical proof," there are multiple versions of the theories and methods that underlie this type of research approach. See, for example, Patricia Ann Lather, *Getting Smart: Feminist Research and Pedagogy With/In the Postmodern* (New York: Routledge, 1991); Joseph Maxwell, *Qualitative Research Design: An Interactive Approach* (Thousand Oaks, CA: Sage Publications, 1996); Max Van Manen, *Researching Lived Experience: Human Science for an Action Sensitive Pedagogy* (Albany: State University of New York Press, 1990); Henry F. Walcott, *Writing Up Qualitative Research* (Newbury Park, CA: Sage Publications, 1990); George Spindler, *Doing the Ethnography of Schooling: Educational Anthropology in Action* (New York: Holt, Reinhart, and Winston, 1982); Robert Bogdan, *Qualitative Research For Education: An Introduction to Theory and Methods* (Boston: Allyn and Bacon, 1982); Sharon B. Merrian, *Case Study Research in Education: A Qualitative Approach* (San Francisco: Jossey-Bass Publishing Co., 1988); I. E. Seidman, *Interviewing as Qualitative Research: A Guide for Researchers in Education and the Social Sciences* (New York: Teachers College Press, 1991).

8   See Lawrence Cremin, "The Nature and Uses of Knowledge," in *American Education: The Metropolitan Experience, 1876–1980* (New York: Harper and Row, 1988) pp. 379–425; John Dewey, *Philosophy and Education in Their Historic Relations*, ed. J. J. Chamblis (Boulder: Westview Press, 1993); Walter Feinberg, *Reason and Rhetoric: The*

Intellectual Foundations of 20th Century Liberal Education Policy (New York: Wiley and Sons, 1975).

9   Studies of design education that were undertaken via funding by the Carnegie Corporation, the Mellen Foundation, the Association of Collegiate Schools of Architecture, or the American Institute of Architecture began in 1929. For an overview of previous studies see Mellen Foundation, *Architecture Education Study Volume 1: The Papers* (Cambridge, MA: Publications Program, Laboratory of Architecture and Planning, Massachusetts Institute of Technology, 1981). For the most recent of these *funded* studies see Ernest L. Boyer and Lee D. Mitgang, *Building Community: A New Future for Architecture Education and Practice* (Princeton: Carnegie Foundation for the Advancement of Teaching, 1996). In his *Voices in Architectural Education* Thomas Dutton asserted the need to explore new sets of teaching issues that included cultural and social issues, multiculturalism, the politics of hidden curriculum, and the marginalization of women and minorities in design studios. See Thomas Dutton, ed., *Voices in Architectural Education: Cultural Politics and Pedagogy* (New York: Bergin and Garvey, 1991).

10 See Clifford Geertz, *The Interpretation of Cultures; Selected Essays* (New York: Basic Books, 1973).

11 For discussions on teacher theory as it emerges within teacher narratives of practice see Sara Lawrence-Lightfoot and Jessica Hoffmann Davis, *The Art and Science of Portraiture* (San Francisco: Jossey-Bass, 1997); Mary Renck Jalongo, *Teachers' Stories: From Personal Narrative to Professional Insight* (San Francisco: Jossey-Bass Publishers, 1995); William Schubert and William Ayers, eds., *Teachers Lore: Learning from Our Own Experience* (New York: Longman, 1992); Joe Kincheloe, *Teachers as Researchers: Qualitative Inquiry as a Path to Empowerment* (New York: Falmer Press, 1991).

Chapter Four: Manny: The Territory of Objectivity

1   Bruce Gurney has investigated the preconceived image of the teacher that students hold as they interact with their present teacher. Following a constructivist approach to teaching and learning, Gurney analyzed students' metaphors for the teaching/learning processes and concluded that the attitudes and beliefs that students carry with them can become reference points for reflection on new meanings that emerge within current interactions. See Bruce Gurney, "Tugboats and Tennis Games: Preconceptions of Teaching and Learning through Metaphor" (Paper presentation, 63rd Annual Meeting of the National Association for Research in Science Teaching, Atlanta, GA, April 1990).

2   The modern version of Plato's objective poetic form is what T.S. Eliot
     explores in his "Impersonal theory of poetry." Eliot follows in the Pla-
     tonic tradition of thinking that the poet objectifies reality through poem
     making. Eliot describes his "Impersonal theory of poetry," writing, "The
     mind of the poet is the shred of platinum. It may partly or exclusively
     operate upon the experience of the man himself; but, the more perfect
     the artist, the more completely separate in him will be the man who suf-
     fers and the mind which creates; the more perfectly will the mind digest
     and transmute the passions which are its materials." See T. S. Eliot,
     "Tradition and the Individual Talent," in *T. S. Eliot: Selected Essays*
     (New York: Harcourt, Brace and Company, 1950) pp. 7–8.

3   William James, *Talks to Teachers on Psychology and to Students on
     Some of Life's Ideals* (New York: W. W. Norton and Company, 1958) pp.
     150–151.

4   William James, *Talks to Teachers*, 150.

5   See Howard Gardner, *Frames of Mind: The Theory of Multiple
     Intelligences* (New York, Basic Books, Inc., 1983).

6   In an insightful essay entitled, "Border Pedagogy in the Age of Postmod-
     ernism," Henry A. Giroux raises the same kinds of questions about the
     usefulness of narratives that support teaching practices that marginalize
     student voices based on the traditional cultural idea that the only legiti-
     mate from of knowledge is objective knowledge. As an alternative to
     traditional pedagogy based on "modernism's reliance on metaphysical
     notions of the subject," Giroux calls for a "border pedagogy [that] both
     confirms and critically engages the knowledge and experience through
     which students author their own voices and construct social identities."
     See Henry A. Giroux, "Border Pedagogy in the Age of Postmodernism,"
     Journal of Education [Boston University] 170 (1988): 162, 175.

Chapter Five: Joe: Listening For Their Vocabularies

1   For more about the collaborative critique type mode for assessing designs
     within professional architectural practice, see Dana Cuff, "Design Prob-
     lems in Practice," in *Architecture: The Story of Practice* (Cambridge, MA:
     MIT Press, 1991) pp. 57–108.

2   That part of the design process in which the designer attempts to "figure
     it out like a puzzle" has been explored by John Archea, who writes, "In
     an attempt to characterize the architect's uncommon mode of action, I
     suggest that the most fundamental aspects of architectural design can best
     be described as a process of "puzzle making." Instead of specifying what
     they are trying to accomplish independently of and prior to their at-
     tempts to accomplish it, as problem-solvers do, architects treat design as a
     search for the most appropriate effects that can be attained in specific spa-

tio-temporal contexts which are in virtually all respects unique." See John Archea, "Puzzle-Making: What Architects Do When No One Is Looking," in Yehuda E. Kalay, ed., *Computability by Design* (New York: A Wiley-Interscience Publication, John Wiley and Sons, 1987) pp. 40–41.

3   Richard Rorty, *Contingency, irony, and solidarity* (New York: Cambridge University Press, 1989) pp. 12–13.

4   Thomas Barone, "Breaking the Mold: The New American Student as Strong Poet," *Theory Into Practice* 32 (Autumn 1993): 239.

5   Nelson Goodman has explored the idea of making knowledge, or as he calls it, "making worlds," through the process of making descriptions. Goodman writes, "truth of statements and rightness of descriptions, representations, exemplifications, expressions—of design, drawing, diction, rhythm—is primarily a matter of fit: fit to what is referred to in one way or another, or to other renderings, or to modes and manners of organization. The differences between fitting a version to a world or a world to a version, and a version together to other versions fade when the role of versions in making the worlds is seen as ranging beyond the acquiring of true beliefs to the discovering and devising of fit of all sorts." See Nelson Goodman, *Ways of Worldmaking* (Indianapolis: Hackett Press, 1978) p. 138.

6   I draw on the writings of Richard Poirier in making my assertion that "the power of language is based on its susceptibility to interpretation," especially his *comparison* of Robert Frost's use of the vague in poetry *to* William James's interest in "the reinstatement of the vague to its proper place in our mental life." In the Jamesian theory of "radical empiricism," *everything* experienced was a legitimate source of making knowledge, even moments of vague feelings, incomplete thoughts, daydreams, or distractions. Poirier relates the kinds of vague experiences that James wanted to reinstate into theorizing the mind *to* kinds of vague poetic expressions like the inconclusive *something* that does not love fences in "Mending Wall." See Richard Poirier's "The Reinstatement of the Vague," in *Poetry and Pragmatism* (Cambridge, MA: Harvard University Press, 1992) pp. 129–168.

7   Richard Coyne and Adrian Snodgrass, "Is designing mysterious? challenging the dual knowledge thesis." *Design Studies* 12 (July 1991): 128.

8   See Eudora Welty, *One Writer's Beginning* (Cambridge, MA: Harvard University Press, 1984).

9   My analysis of teaching practices that emphasize "listening for his students' stories, and vocabularies within their attempt at making their felt inner lives known," draws on the writings of Mary Clare Powell who describes the role of teachers' "inner lives" within creative making processes and curriculum design. See Mary Clare Powell, "The Arts and

the Inner Lives of Teachers," *Phi Delta Kappan* 78 (February 1997): 450–
453.

Chapter Six: Gina: The Complexity of Difference

1   See Harold Bloom, *The Anxiety of Influence: A Theory of Poetry* (New
York: Oxford University Press, 1973).

2   Discrepancies between speakers' and listeners' understandings of one another's meanings (which I call "metaphoric dissonance") have been
explored through qualitative as well as quantitative analyses. For an example of a qualitative analysis on the subject, see Deborah Tannen, *You
Just Don't Understand: Women and Men in Conversations* (New York:
Morrow, 1990) *and* her article "How Men and Women Use Language Differently in Their Lives and in the Classroom," *Educational Digest*
57(February 1992). For a quantitative approach to what sociologists have
termed "discourse analysis," see Gillian Brown, *Speakers, Listeners, and
Communication: Explorations in Discourse Analysis* (New York: Cambridge University Press, 1995).

Chapter Seven: For the Beginnings

1   See Vitruvius, *Vitruvius, The Ten Books on Architecture,* trans. Morris
Hicky Morgan (New York: Dover Publications, 1960).

2   The nonlinearity of design problem solving (which I describe as a process
in which there are "no straight line paths") has been variously explored.
Horst Rittel described design problem nonlinearity in terms of design
problems being "wicked" in the sense that design solutions are indeter-
minate at the start of the process and at the end are a result of social or
psychological factors, rather than logic or prescriptive procedures. See
Horst Rittel, "Dilemmas in a General Theory of Planning," *Policy
Sciences* 4 (1973): 155–169. Herbert Simon describes design problem
nonlinearity in terms of being "ill structured." See Herbert Simon, "The
Structure of Ill-Structured Problems," in Nigel Cross, ed., *Development
in Design Methodology* (New York: John Wiley and Sons, 1984) pp. 145–
166. Jean-Pierre Protzen has explored the contrasts between the various
approaches to design problem solving. See Jean-Pierre Protzen,
"Reflections on the Fable of the Caliph, the Ten Architects and the Philosopher," *Journal of Architectural Education,* 34.

3   For an elaboration of the experiential processes in which "coherent con-
summations" emerge only as conclusions are reached, see John Dewey,
"Having an Experience," in *Art as Experience* (New York: Perigee Press,
1980) p. 38. Dewey writes, "in an experience of thinking, premises
emerge only as a conclusion becomes manifest. The experience, like that
of watching a storm reach its height and gradually subside, is one of continuous movement of subject-matters. Like the ocean in the storm, there

are a series of waves; suggestions reaching out and being broken in a clash, or being carried onwards by a cooperative wave. If a conclusion is reached, it is that of a movement of anticipation and cumulation, one that finally comes to completion. A 'conclusion' is no separate and independent thing; it is the consummation of a movement."

4 Howard Gardner and Thomas Hatch contrasted the traditional views that educators had in assessing student intelligence with the premises that underlay the multiple-intelligence view that Gardner developed in his earlier work entitled *Frames of Mind: The Theory of Multiple Intelligences,* For a discussion that illustrates the contrasts between the traditional and nontraditional theories of intelligence and their application within educational settings, see Howard Gardner and Thomas Hatch, "Multiple Intelligences Go to School," *Educational Researcher* 18 (Nov. 1989): 4–10.

5 See Mike Martin, ""A Beginning Course in Environmental Design: A Humanist Approach," in *Fostering Creativity in Architectural Education, Proceedings of the ACSA West Central Conference* (conference held at University of Illinois at Urbana-Champagne, 1986) p. 102.

6 Stefani Ledewitz, "Discovery, Creativity, and Play," in *Fostering Creativity in Architectural Education, Proceedings of the ACSA West Central Conference* (conference held at University of Illinois at Urbana-Champagne, 1986) p. 122.

7 Amos Rapoport, "Architectural education: there is an urgent need to reduce or eliminate the dominance of the studio," *Architectural Record,* 172 (October 1984): 102.

8 I draw on Richard Rorty's writings in thinking of "seventeenth century astronomic publications as one of many genres of literature that emerged during that era." Rorty contrasts the "scientific philosophies" (that had not abandoned the need for an external God) with Pragmatism, which "does not erect Science as an idol to fill the place once held by God. It views science as one genre of literature—or, put the other way around, literature and the arts as inquiries, on the same footing as scientific inquiries." See Richard Rorty, *Consequences of Pragmatism* (Minneapolis: University on Minnesota Press, 1982) p. xliii. For further reading on the relationship between Science, God, and Pragmatism, see Rorty's *Philosophy and the Mirror of Nature* (Princeton: Princeton University Press, 1979).

9 William James, "A World of Pure Experience," *Essays in Radical Empiricism* (Cambridge, MA: Harvard University Press, 1976) p. 21.

10 Robert Venturi and Denise Scott Brown, who many consider the original pioneers of "postmodern architecture," for example, asserted that their method of discovering the "complex order" of Las Vegas "strip" architec-

ture resulted in the "requiem for the irrelevant works of Art which are today's descendants of a once meaningful Modern architecture": that the discovery of a set of "ordinary" architectural elements that defined the "order" behind the "chaos" of Las Vegas architecture could become the template for a new vocabulary that would replace the old Modern "functionalist" vocabulary. See Robert Venturi and Denise Scott Brown, "A Significance for A&P Parking Lots or Learning From Las Vegas," *Architectural Forum* (March 1968): 91.

11   Elaine Scarry discusses the "creation of the self" as it relates to contemporary theories of knowledge and truth in her insightful essay "The Made-Up and the Made-Real," *Yale Journal of Criticism* Vol. 5, No. 2 (1992): 239–249.

12   Richard Shusterman discusses the philosophical content of the types of popular forms of expression that our younger generation brings to the educative process in his essay, "Rap Remix: Pragmatism, Postmodernism, and Other Issues in the House" *Critical Theory* 20 (Summer 1994). For an in-depth discussion see Richard Shusterman, *Pragmatist Aesthetics: Living Beauty, Rethinking Art* (Cambridge, MA: Blackwell, 1992). Also see Peter Sacks, *Generation X Goes to College: An Eye-Opening Account of Teaching in Postmodern America* (Chicago: Open Court, 1996).

References

Archea, John, "Puzzle-Making: What Architects Do When No One Is Looking." In *Computability By Design*, ed. Yehuda E. Kalay. New York: A Wiley-Interscience Publication, John Wiley and Sons, 1987, pp. 40–41.

Ariew, Roger, and Marjorie Grene eds. *Descartes and His Contemporaries: Meditations, Objections, and Replies.* Chicago: University of Chicago Press, 1995.

Barone, Thomas. "Breaking the Mold: The New American Student as Strong Poet," In *Theory Into Practice* 32, Autumn 1993, pp. 236–243.

Barth, Roland S. *Run School Run.* Cambridge, MA: Harvard University Press, 1980.

Bloom, Harold. *The Anxiety of Influence: A Theory of Poetry.* New York: Oxford University Press, 1973.

Bogdan, Robert. *Qualitative Research For Education: An Introduction to Theory and Methods.* Boston: Allyn and Bacon, 1982.

Bordo, Susan. *Unbearable Weight: Feminism, Western Culture, and the Body.* Berkeley: University of California Press, 1993.

Boyer, Ernest L., and Lee D. Mitgang. *Building Community: A New Future for Architecture Education and Practice.* Princeton: Carnegie Foundation for the Advancement of Teaching, 1996.

Brodkey, Linda, and Michelle Fine. "Presence of Mind in the Absence of Body." In *Journal of Education [Boston University]* 170, 1988, pp. 84–99.

Brown, Gillian. *Speakers, Listeners, and Communication: Explorations in Discourse Analysis.* New York: Cambridge University Press, 1995.

Brown, Harold I. *Rationality.* New York: Routledge, 1988.

Childs, John L. *Education and Morals: An Experimentalist Philosophy of Education.* New York: Appleton-Century-Crofts, Inc., 1950.

Coles, Robert. "On the Nature of Character: Some Preliminary Field Notes." In *Daedalus*, 110, Fall 1981, pp. 131–143.

Compton, Arthur Holly. *The Human Meaning of Science.* Chapel Hill: University of North Carolina Press, 1940.

Coyne, Richard and Adrian Snodgrass. "Is designing mysterious? challenging the dual knowledge thesis." In *Design Studies* 12, July 1991, pp. 124–131.

Cremin, Lawrence. "The Nature and Uses of Knowledge." In *American Education: The Metropolitan Experience, 1876–1980.* New York: Harper and Row, 1988, pp.

Cuff, Dana. "Design Problems in Practice." In *Architecture: The Story of Practice.* Cambridge, MA: MIT Press, 1991.

Darwin, Charles. *On the Origins of Species by Means of Natural Selection.* London: John Murry, 1859.

Dennett, Daniel. *Consciousness Explained.* Boston: Little, Brown and Company, 1991.

Derrida, Jacques. "Structure, Sign, and Play in the Discourse of the Human Sciences." In *Writing and Difference,* trans. Alan Bass, Chicago: University of Chicago Press, 1978, pp. 287–293.

Dewey, John. *The Influence of Darwin on Philosophy.* New York: Holt and Company, 1910.

_____. *How We Think: A Restatement of the Relation of Reflective Thinking to the Educative Process.* Boston: Heath, 1933.

_____. *Experience and Nature.* New York: Dover Publications, Inc., 1958.

_____. "Philosophy." In *Encyclopedia of the Social Sciences Vol. II,* ed. Edwin R. A. Seligman, New York: Macmillan Company, 1962, p. 128.

_____. *Art as Experience.* New York: Perigee Books, 1980.

_____. *Quest For Certainty, John Dewey: The Later Works, 1925–1958 Vol. 12: 1938.* Jo Ann Boydston, ed., Carbondale, IL: Southern Illinois University Press, 1991.

_____. *Philosophy and Education in their Historic Relations.* J. J. Chamblis, ed., Boulder: Westview Press, 1993.

Dutton, Thomas, ed. *Voices In Architectural Education: Cultural Politics and Pedagogy.* New York: Bergin and Garvey, 1991.

Edmundson, Mark. *Literature Against Philosophy: From Plato to Derrida, a Defense of Poetry.* Cambridge [England]: Cambridge University Press, 1995.

Eisner, Elliot W. "On the Differences Between Scientific and Artistic Approaches to Qualitative Research." In *Educational Researcher* 10, April 1981, pp. 5–9.

_____. *The Enlightened Eye: Qualitative Inquiry and the Enhancement of Educational Practice.* New York: Macmillan Publishing Co., 1991.

Eliot, T. S. *T. S. Eliot: Selected Essays.* New York: Harcourt, Brace and Company, 1950.

Feinberg, Walter. *Reason and Rhetoric: The Intellectual Foundations of 20th Century Liberal Education Policy.* New York: Wiley and Sons, 1975.

_____ and Jonas F. Soltis. *School and Society.* New York: Teachers College Press, 1985.

Foucault, Michel. *The History of Sexuality.* Trans. Robert Hurley, New York: Vintage Press, 1978.

Frost, Robert. "Education by Poetry," In *Selected Prose of Robert Frost*, Hyde Cox and Edward Connery Lathem, eds., San Francisco: Holt, Reinhart and Winston, 1966, pp. 33–46.

_____. "Mending Wall." In *The Poetry of Robert Frost: The Collected Poems, Complete and Unabridged*, Edward Connery Lathem, ed., New York: Henry Holt and Company, Owl Books edition, 1979, pp. 33–34.

Galilei, Galileo. *Dialogue Concerning the Two Chief World Systems.* Trans. Stillman Drake, Berkeley: University of California Press, 1953.

Gardner, Howard. *Frames Of Mind: The Theory of Multiple Intelligences* (New York, Basic Books, Inc., 1983).

_____, and Thomas Hatch. "Multiple Intelligences Go to School." In *Educational Researcher* 18, Nov. 1989, pp. 4–10.

Gilligan, Carol, Lyn Mikel Brown, and Annie G. Rogers. "The Psyche Embedded: A Place for Body, Relationships, and Culture in Personality Theory." Monograph #4, Cambridge, MA: Harvard University Laboratory of Human Development, 1988.

Gingerich, Owen. *The Great Copernicus Chase and Other Adventures in Astronomical History.* Cambridge, MA: Sky Publications Corporation, an affiliate of Cambridge [England] University Press 1992.

Giroux, Henry A. "Border Pedagogy In The Age of Postmodernism." In *Journal of Education [Boston University]* 170, 1988, pp. 162–181.

Goodman, Nelson. *Ways of Worldmaking,* Indianapolis: Hackett Press, 1978.

Gurney, Bruce. "Tugboats and Tennis Games: Preconceptions of Teaching and Learning through Metaphor." Paper presentation, 63rd Annual Meeting of the National Association for Research in Science Teaching, Atlanta, GA, April 1990.

Jackson, Philip W. "Secondary Schooling for Children of the Poor." In *Daedalus*, 110, Fall 1981, pp. 39–57.

_____. "Comprehending a Well-Run Comprehensive: A Report on a Visit to a Large Suburban High School." In *Daedalus*, 110, Fall 1981, pp. 81–95.

_____. "Secondary Schooling for the Privileged Few: A Report on a Visit to a New England Boarding School." In *Daedalus*, 110, Fall 1981, pp. 117–130.

Jagger, Allison M. and Susan R. Bordo, eds. *Gender/Body/Knowledge*. New Brunswick, NJ: Rutgers University Press, 1989.

Jalongo, Mary Renck. *Teachers' Stories: From Personal Narrative to Professional Insight*. San Francisco: Jossey-Bass Publishers, 1995.

James, William. *Talks to Teachers on Psychology and to Students on Some of Life's Ideals*. New York: W. W. Norton and Company, 1958.

_____. *Essays in Radical Empiricism*. Cambridge, MA: Harvard University Press, 1976.

Johnson, Mark. *The Body in the Mind, The Bodily Basis of Meaning, Imagination and Reason*. Chicago: University of Chicago Press, 1987.

Kilpatrick, William Heard. *Foundations of Method: Informal Talks on Teaching*. New York: The Macmillan Company, 1925.

Kincheloe, Joe. *Teachers as Researchers: Qualitative Inquiry as a Path to Empowerment*. New York: Falmer Press, 1991.

Kozol, Jonathan. *Death at an Early Age*. New York: Bantam Press, 1968.

Kuhn, Thomas. *The Copernican Revolution; Planetary Astronomy in the Development of Western Thought*. Cambridge, MA: Harvard University Press, 1957.

_____. *The Structure of Scientific Revolutions*, 2nd ed. Chicago: University of Chicago Press, 1970.

Langer, Susanne K. *Mind: An Essay on Human Feeling, Vol. 1*. Baltimore: Johns Hopkins University Press, 1976.

Lather, Partricia Ann. *Getting Smart: Feminist Research and Pedagogy With/In the Postmodern*. New York: Routledge, 1991.

Lawrence-Lightfoot, Sara. "Portraits of Exemplary Secondary Schools: George Washington Carver Comprehensive School." In *Daedalus,* 110, Fall 1981, pp. 17–37.

_____. "Portraits of Exemplary Secondary Schools: Highland Park." In *Daedalus,* 110, Fall 1981, pp. 59–80.

_____. "Portraits of Exemplary Secondary Schools: St. Paul's School." In *Daedalus,* 110, Fall 1981, pp. 97–116.

_____, and Jessica Hoffmann Davis. *The Art And Science Of Portraiture.* San Francisco: Jossey-Bass, 1997.

Laudan, Larry. *Science and Relativism: Some Key Controversies in the Philosophy of Science.* Chicago: University of Chicago Press, 1990.

Ledewitz, Stefani. "Discovery, Creativity, and Play." In *Fostering Creativity in Architectural Education, Proceedings of the ACSA West Central Conference,* held at University of Illinois at Urbana-Champagne, 1986, pp. 119–129.

Lewis, Clarence Irving. *Mind and the World-Order.* New York: Dover, 1929.

Lloyd, Elisabeth A. "Objectivity and the Double Standard for Feminist Epistemologies." In *Synthese* 104, 1995, pp. 351–381

Martin, Mike. "A Beginning Course In Environmental Design: A Humanist Approach." In *Fostering Creativity in Architectural Education, Proceedings of the ACSA West Central Conference,* held at University of Illinois at Urbana-Champagne, 1986, pp.

Maxwell, Joseph. *Qualitative Research Design: An Interactive Approach.* Thousand Oaks, CA: Sage Publications, 1996.

Mellen Foundation. *Architecture Education Study Volume 1: The Papers* (Cambridge, MA: Publications Program, Laboratory of Architecture and Planning, Massachusetts Institute of Technology, 1981.

Merrian, Sharon B. *Case Study Research in Education: A Qualitative Approach.* San Francisco: Jossey-Bass Publishing Co., 1988.

Minsky, Marvin. *The Society of Mind.* New York: Simon and Schuster, 1986.

Nagel, Ernest, Sylvain Bromberger and Adolf Grunbaum, *Observation and Theory in Science.* Baltimore: Johns Hopkins University Press, 1971.

Paley, Vivian Gussin. *White Teacher.* Cambridge, MA: Harvard University Press, 1979.

Poirier, Richard. "The Reinstatement of the Vague." In *Poetry and Pragmatism*. Cambridge, MA: Harvard University Press, 1992, pp. 129–168.

Popper, Karl. *Conjecture and Refutation*. New York: Basic Books, 1962.

_____. *The Logic of Scientific Discovery*. New York: Routledge, 1992.

Powell, Mary Clare. "The Arts and the Inner Lives of Teachers." In *Phi Delta Kappan*, 78, February 1997. pp. 450–453.

Protzen, See Jean-Pierre. "Reflections on the Fable of the Caliph, the Ten Architects and the Philosopher." In *Journal of Architectural Education*, 34.

Putnam, Hilary. *Realism and Reason*. Cambridge [England]: Cambridge University Press, 1983.

_____. *Realism with a Human Face*. Cambridge, MA: Harvard University Press, 1990.

Rapoport, Amos. "Architectural education: "There is an urgent need to reduce or eliminate the dominance of the studio" In *Architectural Record*, 172, Oct. 1984, pp. 102–103.

Rittel, Horst. "Dilemmas in a General Theory of Planning." In *Policy Sciences* 4, 1973, pp. 155–169.

Rorty, Richard. *Consequences of Pragmatism*. Minneapolis: University on Minnesota Press, 1982.

_____. *Contingency, irony, and solidarity*. New York: Cambridge University Press, 1989.

_____. *Philosophy and the Mirror of Nature*. Princeton: Princeton University Press, 1990.

_____. *Objectivity, relativism, and truth*. New York: Cambridge University Press, 1991.

Rugg, Harold. *Culture and Education in America*. New York: Harcourt, Brace and Company, 1931.

Sacks, Peter. *Generation X Goes to College: An Eye-Opening Account of Teaching in Postmodern America*. Chicago: Open Court, 1996.

Scarry, Elaine. "The Made-Up and the Made-Real." *Yale Journal of Criticism*, 5.2, 1992, pp. 239–249.

Scheffler, Israel. *Science and Subjectivity*. Indianapolis: Hackett Publishing Co., 1982.

Schön, Donald A. "The Architectural Studio as an Exemplar of Education for Reflection-in-Action." In *Journal of Architectural Education* 38, Fall 1984, pp. 2–9.

_____. *Educating the Reflective Practitioner.* San Francisco: Jossey-Bass Publishers, 1987.

Schubert, William, and William Ayers, eds. *Teachers Lore: Learning from Our Own Experience.* New York: Longman, 1992.

Searle, John. *The Rediscovery of the Mind,* Cambridge, MA: MIT Press, 1992.

_____. "Rationality and Realism, What Is at Stake?" In *Daedalus,* 122, Fall 1993, pp. 55–83.

Seidman, I. E. *Interviewing as Qualitative Research: A Guide for Researchers in Education and the Social Sciences.* New York: Teachers College Press, 1991.

Shusterman, Richard. *Pragmatist Aesthetics: Living Beauty, Rethinking Art.* Cambridge, MA: Blackwell, 1992.

_____, Rap Remix: Pragmatism, Postmodernism, and Other Issues in the House." In *Critical Theory* 20, Summer 1994.

Simon, Herbert. "The Structure of Ill-Structured Problems." In *Development in Design Methodology,* Nigel Cross, ed., New York: John Wiley and Sons, 1984.

Spindler, George. *Doing the Ethnography of Schooling: Educational Anthropology in Action.* New York: Holt, Reinhart, and Winston, 1982.

Tannen, Deborah. *You Just Don't Understand: Women and Men in Conversations.* New York: Morrow, 1990.

_____. "How Men and Women Use Language Differently in Their Lives and in the Classroom." In *Educational Digest* 57, Feb. 1992.

Turing, A. M. "Can a Machine Think?" In *The World of Mathematics,* James R. Newman, ed., New York: Simon and Schuster, 1956, pp. 2099–2123.

Van Manen, Max. *Researching Lived Experience: Human Science for an Action Sensitive Pedagogy.* Albany: State University of New York Press, 1990.

Venturi, Robert and Denise Scott Brown. "A Significance for A&P Parking Lots or Learning from Las Vegas." In *Architectural Forum,* March 1968 36–43, 89, 91.

Vitruvius [Vitruvius Pollio] *Vitruvius, The Ten Books on Architecture.* Morris Hicky Morgan, translator. New York: Dover Publications, 1960.

Walcott, Henry F. *Writing Up Qualitative Research.* Newbury Park, CA: Sage Publications, 1990.

Welty, Eudora. *One Writer's Beginnings.* Cambridge, MA: Harvard University Press, 1984.

Westbrook, Robert. *John Dewey and American Democracy.* Ithaca, NY: Cornell University Press, 1991.

White, Hayden. "The Value of Narrativity in the Representation of Reality," *The Content of the Form.* Baltimore: Johns Hopkins University Press, 1987, pp. 1–25.

Index

About the Author

Photo by Lisa Lazaro

Elijah Mirochnik is Assistant Professor in the Creative Arts in Learning Division at Lesley College in Cambridge, Massachusetts. He received his Ph.D. in architecture from the University of California at Berkeley. His numerous innovative and experimental curriculum designs stem from his research in the areas of interracial classroom collaboration, teacher construction of identity, and student artistic expression of social responsibility.

Studies in the Postmodern Theory of Education

General Editors
Joe L. Kincheloe & Shirley R. Steinberg

Counterpoints publishes the most compelling and imaginative books being written in education today. Grounded on the theoretical advances in criticalism, feminism, and postmodernism in the last two decades of the twentieth century, Counterpoints engages the meaning of these innovations in various forms of educational expression. Committed to the proposition that theoretical literature should be accessible to a variety of audiences, the series insists that its authors avoid esoteric and jargonistic languages that transform educational scholarship into an elite discourse for the initiated. Scholarly work matters only to the degree it affects consciousness and practice at multiple sites. Counterpoints' editorial policy is based on these principles and the ability of scholars to break new ground, to open new conversations, to go where educators have never gone before.

For additional information about this series or for the submission of manuscripts, please contact:

Joe L. Kincheloe & Shirley R. Steinberg
637 West Foster Avenue
State College, PA 16801

To order other books in this series, please contact our Customer Service Department at:

(800) 770-LANG (within the U.S.)
(212) 647-7706 (outside the U.S.)
(212) 647-7707 FAX

or browse online by series at:
www.peterlang.com

anyone. I had curfews, and it was "so juvenile!" Well tough luck—that's the law, and that's the way I want it. She would go off to people's apartments and I was real negative on that. Now that I know her friends a little better and I know that I can't change her going with them without physically dragging her out, I'm adjusting. But it is a little difficult thinking of her seeing guys who are six years older than she is. But she is a mature person. I don't know. . . .

When Xia was in grade one, her teacher suggested that she skip a grade because she was so advanced. But she already had a late birthday, and I thought they shouldn't be pushing. She should grow up with kids her own age. She'd be shorter [than the others in her class]! Her grandparents were pushing it. But these last few months I've been thinking that it wouldn't have been a bad thing.

Xia spent a lot of her time with her friends, who were mainly older than she was. Most of them were male, but she also had close female friends at school and one older female confidant who had left school a few years before. She said that they liked to go to a coffee shop and talk until 3:00 or 4:00 A.M. Xia's mother was concerned: "I worry about the influence of these older boys. It is not so much Xia's judgment about being with them; it is their ideas that they put into her head, and all of a sudden that becomes important to her. Maybe that is where she remains a teenager."

Despite personal conflicts, Xia never denied that she was a successful student, unlike many other young women, who felt that personal problems somehow negated their school achievements. She had the ability to separate her private life from her public life, and she had confidence in doing that.

End Thoughts

Xia's notions of success were exemplified by her outstanding performances onstage, her ability to write and communicate effectively, and the teachers and students who thought of her as a success. She often spoke of school as a means to an end. She sought and received counseling from the school social worker; she was a public figure, like Alexis, and was well-known around the school. She circumvented her problems with the school, for example, by auditioning for and being accepted by a community theater. She went elsewhere to get what she wanted, and that was to act. She bypassed obstacles preventing her from getting where she wanted to go—to a liberal arts college specializing in theater. She did not do her detentions after school, and she got away with it.

Contrary to Werner's (1989) finding that just being at school is a protective factor, she skipped a lot of school to do her work at home and to visit with her friends who were not in school.

Xia was very much influenced by her close circle of friends, who were strong believers in the philosophy of "fulfillment of the whole person," and this included caring for other people, which she did as a peer counselor.

Her extended family gave her support in the form of both financial aid and encouragement.

Xia tapped into the politics of the school very well. She established her credit with teachers by scoring well on standardized tests and performing brilliantly on stage. They were prepared to give her a lot of liberty because of her perceived successes. She was a calculating manipulator of the system, and this worked very well for her. There was a lot of tolerance of her behavior on the part of the school. But toward the end of the school year, this tolerance was wearing thin.

Chapter 8

Not Your Usual Success Story

The young women in this study were all different. Their differences bespoke their ethnic backgrounds, SES, position in the family, family stressors, and a multitude of personality and individual differences. They did not fit the usual success story. The preceding descriptive chapters are meant to give the reader an insight into the interplay of the young women's biographies and the ways they went about becoming academically successful. This chapter examines the processes these five young women used to become successful when circumstances stood in the way of their success. The understandings are interpreted within three frameworks: the self-as-agent for success, the way the families functioned to achieve success, and the way the students worked the school to achieve success. Rather than designating one context—for example, the family or the school—as an at-risk or a protective factor in a student's life, I have looked for strengths and weakness in all contexts to discover how students use strengths and perceive failure across all settings.

The Self-as-Agent

Agency, as I use the term, is the ability to be instrumental in achieving an end or in influencing the process of becoming something. Bandura's (1977) notion of self-efficacy (as described in chapter 1) is unconvincing as an explanation for the academic success of these five young women. Bandura included contextual factors in his analysis of self, but they tend to stand on their own; they cannot be seen as intimately linked to and extending across contexts of family and school. Benhabib's (1992) notion of the self-as-agent, reported in chapter 1, is less deterministic and better able to express a person's movement across contextual boundaries. The tendency of critical theorists to ignore the personal while focusing on the structural leaves a critical gap in the construction of knowledge. This study places the personal and structural issues side by side to see how the multiple readings create a richer tapestry for greater understanding.

Although these girls were active participants in their families and in school, their approaches to participation were different; still, they were all instrumental in their own academic success. Benard (1992) talked about resilient children being socially competent, possessing problem-solving skills, being autonomous, and having a sense of purpose and future. These five young women possessed all these qualities in varying degrees.

The young women's responsiveness in recognizing opportunities for success is discussed in four ways: taking control and being a leader, channeling stress and anger, focusing on the present and the future, and establishing idiosyncratic credit. In keeping with the original intention to integrate the contexts of family and school, the self-as-agent is discussed in these four contexts.

Taking Control and Being a Leader

School was one area of their lives in which the young women in this study believed they could take control. From their biographies, we see that they had little control over events at home, but at school they had many opportunities to be involved and feel competent. These young women were able to control their lives when they felt they were functioning as adults, and school provided a setting in which they could so function.

For Jasmine, Xia, and Alexis, leadership and involvement at school were opportunities to take control. Each of them belonged to organizations in which they were officeholders.

Jasmine talked about her two lives, one of quiet subservience at home and the other as an outgoing leader of numerous school activities:

> Helping other people is enjoyable. I mean, I know that the entire staff contributes to the newspaper, but when I look at it, I see the outcome is how I organize it, and it kind of reflects on me, you know. I have just started enjoying leadership this year. Being editor is the ultimate accomplishment for me.

Having control over the newspaper and seeing it as a reflection of herself gave Jasmine a sense of belonging and worth. Each